What people are saying about
LAST OF THE PO'RICANS Y
OTROS AFRO-ARTIFACTS

Like a cool glass of water on a hot summer day...no...more like an oasis not a mirage on this desert we call earth...Not4Prophet comes to bring relief...to let you...me...all thinking people know...we are not alone. I can feel that breeze. I welcome it. There must be a sail cloth somewhere which we will hoist and ride until we find...no create...a new world.

— Nikki Giovanni
Poet and scholar

In *Last of the Po'Ricans*, Not4Prophet delivers "The Daily News" of poetry in a Hip Hop beat entangled in blues/plena/rock 'n roll/punk/fusion/folk jazz mixed with explosive emotions crafted into each outburst. He delivers rapid fire political, apolitical, patriotic, treasonous, nationalistic, anti-capitalistic, take it or leave it, fuck it, in your face poetry that excites and incites. As he pays homage to old school cats from the Nuyorican and Black Arts movements, Not4Prophet breaks boundaries with iconic imagery and word play, creating a new school of thought by daring to speak truths we ought to be talking about.

— Jesús Papoleto Meléndez
Nuyorican poet and author of *Hey Yo! Yo Soy!*

The poet's nu, yo, and he's rican as ri can. He claims to be po'rican, and that po is for the poEMS you know, bro, as the rican is rich as a tostones slangwhich. It's all write hear, twixt pages and ear. La tradición. Can't beat it, off the street it's coming through so clear it's all you hear. The air is tattooed, gracias Not4, a Prophet for our time.

— Bob Holman
Poet, professor, cultural activist, founder/proprietor of the
Bowery Poetry Club, and Artistic Director of Bowery Arts + Science

Not4Prophet's *Last of the Po'Ricans*, is a BeBop collage of images that saturate the mind with images of an El Barrio word warrior. It takes you on his trip through the 'hood in his heart and mind with a keen sense of alliteration as his signature.

— Abiodun Oyewole
Poet, teacher and founding member of the
ıerican music and spoken-word group, *The Last Poets*

Beware those who enter here: this poetry burns and it hurts when it burns, yet it is agonizingly beautiful. This is the kind of Nuyorican cum Black Arts movement poetry that speaks not just for but to the voiceless, with urgency and clarity, scribing a reality that many of us live and endure but rarely see in print. With stark, lyrical, and bold illustrations by Vagabond, this volume bears witness to the rhythm, rhyme, grit, grime, and decolonized desire of an uncompromised Boricua aesthetic. Like thunder to lightning, Vagabond's agit-prop artwork creates a powerful visual counterpoint to Not4Prophet's raging verse. An unsettling joy to read and a phenomenal first collection of poems.

— Lisa Sánchez González
Author of *Boricua Literature: A Literary History of the Puerto Rican Diaspora* (NYU Press 2001) and *The Stories I Read to the Children, The Life and Writing of Pure Belpré* (Centro Press, 2013).

In these times of neoliberal barrios and their nuyo-literal MCs, Not4Prophet ups the anti (sic) on us all. There's virtuoso flow here ("cutting umbilical cords / with a subliminal sword") but there's also a restless intelligence attuned to an inclusive Boricua affect that brings together everyone from de Burgos and Basquiat to Lolita Lebrón and Sylvia Rivera in a "puerto punk rock"- and- krylon mixtape. In the spirit of the Nuyorican tradition, this is a poet of the political imagination who is unafraid of keepin' it surreal, leading us beyond the trendy real estate and into the mind-reel of the city as lived. The flow here is anarcho-global ("between the front lines of fanon and magón"), yet these agit-prophecies are less about preaching to the choir than about an improvised explosive verbal energy as boundless as it is shareable—"ad-liberation theologies," the poet calls them. Although it is a first take, *Last of the Po' Ricans y otros afro-artifacts* is already a keeper, its gut-rhymes poised skillfully between revolú and revolution.

— Urayoán Noel
Poet, scholar, and professor at SUNY Albany

The poems in *Last of the Po'Ricans y Otros Afro-artifacts* are intensely lyrical, rhythmic, heart wrenching, raw, painful and hopeful. Simultaneously furious and tender, they echo the song lyrics Not4Prophet wrote as lead singer for Puerto Punk cult band *Ricanstruction* in the 1990s. Alliterating his way into our hearts/minds, Not4Prophet weaves together anything-but-linear poetic narratives with unpredictable twists and turns that are rich in historical and cultural detail. These details are in fact so rich (and often also surprising and rare) that I could only marvel at the ingeniousness of what I was catching while also wondering about everything that was flying over my head. While often relying on dystopian themes and imagery, *Last of the Po'Ricans y Otros afro-artifacts* is at its core deeply committed to freedom, health and wholeness. It represents a strangely fitting way to be utopian in our times.

— Raquel Z. Rivera, independent scholar, singer-songwriter, author of
New York Ricans from the Hip Hop Zone (Palgrave Macmillan, 2003)
and editor of *Reggaton* (Duke University Press, 2009)

Not4Prophet digs deep to unearth a time capsule of sacred and subversive texts delivering poetic justice that transcends boundaries and crosses the intersections of identity, collective belonging and trans-Atlantic dispossession. These lyrical excavations of truth raging and loving and dying against the machine are more valid than any epidemiological surveillance of the health and dis-ease of the Afro-Boriqua diaspora in Nueva York. I am filled with gratitude that this Griot has committed his canon of verses to the page to be properly savored and digested as what should be required reading for all.

— Lynn Roberts
Reproductive Justice Activist/Assistant Professor,
CUNY School of Public Health

What words can be offered a wordsmith who in saying that his words are "grenade pins getting under the thin skins of uncle psalm's cabin" has already said it all. After that there can only be words of encouragement, especially when his words have already encouraged a very necessary "common rebellion."

— Dr. Jared Ball, Associate of Communication Studies,
Morgan State University and author of *I Mix What I Like!: A Mixtape Manifesto*

LAST OF THE PO' RICANS
Y OTROS AFRO-ARTIFACTS

LAST OF THE PO' RICANS Y OTROS AFRO-ARTIFACTS

POEMS BY NOT4PROPHET

GRAPHICS BY VAGABOND
INTRODUCTION BY TONY MEDINA

NEW YORK

www.2leafpress.org

P.O. Box 4378
Grand Central Station
New York, New York 10163-4378
editor@2leafpress.org
www.2leafpress.org

2LEAF PRESS
is an imprint of the
Intercultural Alliance of Artists & Scholars, Inc. (IAAS),
a NY-based nonprofit 501(c)(3) organization that promotes
multicultural literature and literacy.
www.theiaas.org

Cover photo: Jeffrey Akers
Cover design: Richard "Vagabond" Beaumont
Cover concept: Sam Lahoz (http://www.slny.net)
Book design and layout: Gabrielle David
Editors: Carmen Pietri Diaz and Tomás Urayoán Noel

Library of Congress Control Number: 2013937967

ISBN-13: 978-0-9884763-3-2 (Paperback)
ISBN-13: 978-0-9884763-2-5 (eBook)

BISAC: Poetry / Caribbean & Latin America

10   9   8   7   6   5   4   3   2   1

Published in the United States of America

First Edition | First Printing

The publisher wishes to thank the 2Leaf Press crew for a phenomenal job on this book, with special thanks to Vagabond Beaumont who envisioned it.

2LEAF PRESS trade distribution is handled by University of Chicago Press / Chicago Distribution Center (www.press.uchicago.edu) 773.702.7010. Titles are also available for corporate, premium, and special sales. Please direct inquiries to the UCP Sales Department, 773.702.7248.

For my mother María Báez
who taught me to speak...

and my father Pedro Báez
who told me to shout...

and my teachers the NuyoRicans
who took me to school...

"Poetry belongs to everybody" —David Hernandez

"I bear within my soul profound
feelings of love and endearment for
Puerto Rico, and a world of poetry
which could resound like a holocaust
for all its natural splendors."

—Ramón Romero Rosa

"work without bread in this poetry
factory"

—Miguel Piñero

"this is not a joke ...
poetry is serious business"

—Lolita Lebrón

TABLE OF CONTENTS

INTRODUCTION

What Profits a People
Whose Poet Prophesizes?

When tyranny is law
revolution is order.

—Don Pedro Albizu Campos

THE GREAT HARRY BELAFONTE, when inducting the iconic revolutionary Hip Hop group Public Enemy into the Rock & Roll Hall of Fame, referred to them as artists who are "the gatekeepers of Truth and Civilization's radical voice." The same could be said of Not-4Prophet whose poetry and lyrics have consistently challenged paradigms of oppression regarding his people—Boricuas—and oppressed groups globally—giving his voice a sense of urgency and alarm in these precarious times where the super rich continue to conspire to squeeze every bit of life, happiness and joy from the majority of the people on this polluted planet with their undying pedestrian lust for land, resources and profit.

Yet the question becomes: What profits a people whose poet prophesizes? For creation is everything and creators create thinking they can create everything, though we still have despair and children still go hungry and people still are homeless and we still are dying. But what can we create and how can we recreate ourselves so that we will not repeat our miserable fumbles? Ideas constantly flipped and mangled and disentangled in so many jumbled minds; American consumption and consumerism overly—overtly—propagandized to have us constantly ask ourselves: What good is poetry—or revolution, for that matter? That have even the confused among us trapped in a cartoon of apathy, snickering off to some closet or private library creating ads for American economic propaganda, reduced to a laugh from the drunken lame bohemian village lumps and a puzzled bewildered stare from a hungry brown boy and brown girl on a broken Harlem-South Bronx stoop; his own image inverted, slapped back and twisting in his ambivalent gut begging for clarity; for what is necessary and real; for what is true and beautiful and humane; for what will call upon and provoke the death of the greedy and insincere.

Not4Prophet heeds this call—this calling—with his clarion call of a book, a verbal megaphone in all its rough-hewn poetic grace and in-your-face bombast. His *Last of the Po' Ricans* is a James Baldwin *Fire Next Time* warning in all its profound, prophetic glory; a lyrical ghetto beat down from the heart of the 'hood.

The poems herein are not FDA—or MFA—approved. They are not easily palatable—or respectable—for that matter. They do not attempt at a teacup mantelpiece aesthetic that wishes to adorn the parlors of the filthy rich or their aesthete, bourgeois acolytes. They wish to smash class with a battering ram of Hip Hop and Salsa verve, served straight up in a machine gun take-no-prisoners rice-and-beans aesthetic rife with internal rhyme and flashes of imagery that come natural as breathing, that clang and clash, that rumble in the jungle—that tells it like it is—Gil Noble meets Bob Marley meets Hector Lavoe with a rapper's flow-style.

In the tradition of Langston Hughes, Julia de Burgos, Amiri Baraka, Nikki Giovanni, Pedro Pietri, Louis Reyes Rivera, Roque Dalton, Jayne Cortez and Pablo Neruda, Not4Prophet advances a poetics of love and righteous indignation at the plight of his people beholden to the merci-lessness of greed, indifference and profit.

The great guerilla warrior and revolutionist, Che Guevara, once famously said, "The true revolutionary is guided by great feelings of love." Essentially, these are love poems—no matter the ferocity from which these poetic pimp smacks may come, they are in defense of the very poor and exploited; in defiance of despair and the devil-may-care atti-tudes of those yielding economic power; in contradistinction of capital-ism and the unnecessary human misery it brings.

We need more social poets like Not4Prophet who finds in himself a love enough for his community—and the greater globally oppressed community—to use his poetry for what it's supposed to be utilized for—to bear witness to—and ultimately to speak truth to power (in the words of James Baldwin and Mari Evans) by negating the negation of his Black Boricua Nation.

There is no greater honor; no calling more necessary. And he (or she) who engages in such a task is a selfless warrior—and lover—who will reap the benefits and profits from being a prophet in the generation fortunate enough to be blessed by the virtuousness of his voice, vision, valiance and veritable verbiage.

From the bodega sold dreams of Miguel Piñero to the polyphonic Black consciousness of The Last Poets, Not4Prophet's poems do not cauterize the pain suffered by those living at the bottom of society or sliding down what Haitian revolutionary poet Rene Depestre refers to as "the greasy pole" of capitalism. He castigates a dumbed down society hell bent on maintaining its hegemony through complacency, complicity and a deliberate lack of consciousness precipitated by deceit, distortion, distraction and sheer laziness and selfishness. He celebrates the beauty of what the late great Salsero Hector LaVoe called "mi gente."

Not4Prophet's gente are not the boardroom bores who bomb and blast nations with boorish braggadocio, rearranging sovereign nations like cheap Walmart furniture for land and oil, for resources and money, sacrificing blood (seeing humans as capital) and cultures to fill their colonialist coffers. His gente are not the pedantic pork chop preachers or puerile proselytizing politicians and journalists embedded in the asshole hairs of corporate interest or talking heads and so-called educators paid to lie and stretch the truth until it snaps like a dried-out rubber band in the clumsy hands of bullies threatening us with slingshots of disinformation designed to diss us until we disappear.

Not4Prophet's gente are the masses who at times are asses, as the great Pedro Pietri once exclaimed. His gente are those who heed the clarion call and clarity of his lyrical prowess and flow. They are those prophets who have come before him and passed on to him the baton of revolutionary responsibility. They are those to whom he pays homage by reading and recycling their words for the coming generations. They are a roll call of great artists and thinkers who did not dare deceive the people, but demanded clarity as clear as running water. In *Last of the Po' Ricans,* Not4Prophet conjures up and pays homage to his cultural, literary and revolutionary ancestors, calling out and culling together, to gather: Don Pedro Albizu Campos, José Martí, Pedro Pietri, Louis Reyes Rivera, Jayne Cortez, Hector Lavoe, Roberto Clemente, Jean-Michel Basquiat, James Baldwin, Octavio Paz, Paulo Freire, Miguel Piñero, Julia de Burgos and Friedrich Nietzsche.

He calls upon the living by conjuring their words as epigraphs to poems that "reclaim the streets" with "raw reality of rican resistance." Here, we hear from poets as varied as Tato Laviera, Miguel Algarín, Elizabeth Alexander, Bimbo Rivas, Assata Shakur juxtaposed against a Hip Hop landscape of Krylon graffiti, battle rhymes, B-boys and historiographies that takes us back to Taínos and caciques to Operation Bootstrap to the claptrap of Nuyorican reality and surreality.

Not4Prophet points out the absurdity, contradictions and inconsistencies of capitalism and colonialism to those whose mentalities are still stuck in colonialism and slavery. He believes, as he quotes Paulo Freire, that "language is never neutral" and that, as James Baldwin reminds us, "[a] language comes into existence by means of brutal necessity." What Not4Prophet manages to do, as our ancestors in Africa and the Caribbean have historically done, and as our brothers and sisters in the heart of our 'hoods have done with beats and rhymes, is to scratch out a language of collage and clarity that organizes the chaos of capitalism into comprehension in order for the people—his gente—to reap the benefits of his flow(s), as the Puerto Rican maestro Piri Thomas referred to in his poems.

Not4Prophet's *Last of the Po' Ricans* disses the disingenuous and praises the people. It castigates and condemns capitalism and colonialism and its neos and lying griots; it pulls the curtain back to expose the Wizard; it shows us that the Emperor indeed has no clothes. But it also sings a Salsa Blues in Hip Hop harmony. It reminds us, as the great revolutionary poet Roque Dalton, gunned down by an extreme faction of his leftist organization, that "Poetry like bread is for everyone."

Not4Prophet gives us necessary bread and nourishment in the guise of love poems. They are sometimes harsh, sometimes satirical and soothingly reassuring. But they are never ever disingenuous, pompous or positioned or posed as if above the mass. They care about human beings and their livelihoods. They care about the future of the planet and its inhabitants. They are preoccupied with occupying common sense and common decency in order for people to be treated fairly and equitably. These poems be patriotic, they be about justice—for all.

As the late great master poet Gwendolyn Brooks wrote about Jayne Cortez's seminal collection *Coagulations:* "Jayne Cortez is an energy, a nourishment, a Black Nation song." The same can be said of Not4Prophet, but I would humbly modify it to say, " Not4Prophet is 'an energy, a nourishment, a Black [Boricua] song'." Punto, as Piri Thomas would punctuate.

Last of the Po' Ricans signifies to us that this is the last time Ricans will be po'! For a revolution in verse will chant down Babylon. It signals the arrival of a necessary poet on the frontline of that full frontal lobotomy on American culture and autopsy on capitalism. And only the people will profit from the poetry of Not4Prophet.

His gente. *Siempre con la gente.*

—Tony Medina
Poet, Professor and Activist

the prophet of el barrio

"Y cada pueblo libertado era una hazaña del poeta y era un poema del soldado. ¡y fue crucificado …!"

— Luis Lloréns Torres

In a casita on the corner of 138th street and st. ann's in the boogie down bronx on a frozen nueba yo' morning, the porto rican prophet Pedro, son of ghetto guerilla guillermo, imagined by immaculate conception, cradled in the emaciated arms of methadone madonna maría was re-born with a streetlight halo glowing dimly above his fractured skull, sheltered by lost and found splinters of wood and a linoleum scrap roof, a cracked asphalt and dirt floor, stray dogs, alley cats, colonized chickens, a plastic rooster, project pigeons, rebellious rats, a plaster caste santa bárbara, an empty bottle of bacardí, and wrapped in a soiled single starred bandera, the mambo messiah, king of the crackheads, lord of the dope fiends, hope of every casualty on every corner of every calle in every barrio, arrived when he was most needed. The sufferahs had been waiting wanting worrying that he would never see life or touch their lives, suicide visionary, slum still birth boricua, death defying son of a sanctified cemetery sista. But there it stood, looking older than it should for its short time in the slum, an almost world weary gaze that belied a vacant stare-scared squint, a pallid yet porto rican face and broken body covered in blood that looked like mud that looked like dirt that looked like earth, and starch like spit that looked like sewage that tasted like survival and smelled like salvation caked around its tiny clenched mouth. It had been said in bodega bochinche and predicted in project prophecy and carried in the silent stench of the 6 train from the bronx to 116th street in el barrio that pedro of porto rico would roar with a piercing, painful cry like a trapped animal, like a kicking junkie, like a warning of the art-pocalypse that was to come, that was already here, with a saintly scream blues bible baptismal baby shout, the prophet would speak out, and the word would free us all from this world and our real and imaginary chains and corpses — cadenas y cuerpos. So they gathered at the junkyard turned parking lot turned dirt roots garden turned holy land, sitting and standing among the weeds and waste and waited and wondered and worried as the meek became many and many became masses and masses became a mob, they asked gently that the mortuary momma slap the savior so it would cry out, and as a millennium turned to moments and moments to months, they demanded angrily that she hit him hard so that he would scream, and they would hear the chaotic clarion final call and all, but pedro could not take another hit and María would not administer it, and people turned paupers turned parishioners turned priest turned to the police, who claimed cultural custody of the calle crack christ carrying him like a crushed corpse to his waiting squad car cradle cage and charged his mother with the act of clandestine creation. But the prophet had not yet spoken screamed shouted saved or even spit, and the junkies flunkies fakes fanatics and followers wanted him freed from the pontius pilot-lite pigs and themselves saved from the shit stink sickness of sheer slum survival. So they encircled the cops calling and chanting and crying for the release of the colonized christ child, his utterance would be their uprise, his word their weapon, his voice their vision, his roar their re-lease, his predicament their prison.... But the pigs told the people that the child was sick, stricken, small, stunted, docile, damaged, doomed, dying, DOA, and they had no choice but to find a way to take him away and he had nothing to say anyway.... But as the savior stood silent and the people grew violent, and the authorities almost afraid, with arms aimed at the angry agitated and aimless, they stated that the broken battered bastard baby could not stutter, stammer, screech, or squawk, and certainly not talk...and to prove it they pried open his miraculous mouth to reveal a gaping black hole that was his missing tongue....

the great dying (part uno)

"History, history! We fools, what do we know or care? History begins for us with murder and enslavement, not with disvovery."

— William Carlos Williams

Mi mami, the self-described taína, held mi mano gently, but strongly, as we entered into the museum somewhere in the middle of man-hat-tan in a place called nuevo yo. We headed straight for the dry death-room, where we was told by the helpful Hispanic security guard that "the old taíno artifacts was kept for the public viewing for all."

Ab-original rocks; sea shell pendants; carvings of maquetaurie guay-aba, lord of the land of the dead; stone beads; petroglyphs of atabey, the mother goddess and yucahu, the supreme deity cacique skeletons.

Releasing my wrist from mi mami's over-powering fist, I swiftly moved closer to the glass cases that held them x-cavated treasures, so that I could try to read the little fools-gold-colored plaques that would x-plain all about the his-story of them old stolen stones.

"the way they normally dealt with the native leaders and nobles was to tie them to a kind of griddle consisting of sticks resting on pitchforks driven into the ground and then grill them over a slow fire, with the result that they howled in agony and despair as they died a lingering death..."

"these mortal enemies of human/kind trained hunting dogs to track them down – wild dogs who would savage a native to death as soon as look at him, tearing him to shreds and devouring his flesh as though he were a pig..."

"they spared no one, erecting especially wide gibbets on which they could string their victims up with their feet just off the ground and then burn them alive thirteen at a time, in honour of our savior and the twelve apostles, or tie dry straw to their bodies and set fire to it..."

"they slaughtered anyone and everyone in their path, on oc-casion running through a mother and her baby with a single thrust of their swords..."

"they forced their way into native settlements, slaughtering everyone they found there, including small children, old men, pregnant women, and even women who had just given birth. They hacked them to pieces, slicing open their bellies with their swords as though they were so many sheep herded into a pen..."

"they even laid wagers on whether they could manage to slice a man in two at a stroke, or cut an individual's head from his body, or disembowel him with a single blow of their axes..."

"they grabbed suckling infants by the feet and, ripping them from their mothers', breast, dashed them headlong against the rocks..."

"he brought these wretched men to justice and, their crimes being duly attested to, he caused them to be burned alive in public..."

"the remaining prisoners were seized with despair, for they had not escaped with their comrades, and it was discovered the next morning that they had hanged themselves from the bridge-poles..."

"the Indians, forced with the need either to become a lowly, marginalized part of the European colonial system or, as they continue to do in increasing numbers, to perish altogether..."

I looked up at mi mami, the living, breathing taína, with con-fused and con-found-ed wide-wondering-eyes, whispering, tenatively, "mami, it say that the taíno is x-tinct?"

Mi mami stared me dead straight in the face for a long moment, suck-ing her lips in the way that some west indian women sometimes do, took a long, deep breath, grabbed my hand or wrist, again, tighter, this time, and led me out of the mausoleum, and back out on to the streets, and off towards the subway six train that would transport us back uptown and back to our own (el) barrio where we still lived.

mi papi was a nuyorican poem

the way he walked it and talked shit
in sharp switchblade sentences
a barrel-chested barrio bad b-boy
busted bottle of bootlegged bacardí
bullet shot stride from borinquen
to da south boogie down bronx
east harlem via west africa
and attica and back again
and against a nuevo yo
basque blood clot beat down
but unbowed bastard body
covered in jailhouse jesus-che
tat scratches on a cell block
cruci-fix make-shift machetes
and mi mami's fine fractured face
in first draft form fragile but un-torn
scrawled onto his scarred and charred
armed alongside de-faced faded
savage skulls and unbent broken bones
imperfect tone poems of an almost e-raced
ancient alias across india inked fingers
flashed fast into furious FBI terror list fists
that chased away migrant mice
and fought off monster molesters
and them gentle men from man-hattan
who tried to take away our cupones
or vied to cut off mi papi's cultural cojones

3-time loser (Dec 31, 1972)

"To the people here, we are outsiders. Foreigners."

— Roberto Clemente

from three kings to three rivers
to 3 strikes and you're olmos
outshined by white yanquis
in pin-striped suits
spinning spiked spic balls
at black list power fist fouls
off golden wrists
3000 hits and misses
dodging goodbye kisses
swing and found missing
during a managua mercy mission
flying food to earth-quake sir-vivors
sí vera and the three robertitos
waving adiós on new jeers eve
as a DC in 72 carried off precious
cargo and the most valuable prayer
four time battling cham-peon
a bad ass broke bodied
black porto rican chattel
from sugar mill to steel mill
caught by crabbers
and bought by pirates
for 5000 goya beans
paid in stolen bases
and replay races
against foreign faceless racists
fair-weather fan-addicts
and aging bobby-soxers
aching for another home team
champion-ship or a brother-nigga
slave ship to sale numero 21
back home to Borinquen
in a battered box
with a Bithorn in his side

3000

during a managua mercy mission...

slave ship to sale
numero 21 back
home to Borinquen
in a battered box

★ ★ ★ No. 143 ★ ★ ★

Roberto Clemente

PITTSBURGH PIRATES — OUTFIELDER

Ht. 5'11"; Wt. 175; Bats Right; Throws Right;
Born Aug. 18, 1934; Home; Rio Piedras, P. R.
Roberto's most successful major league sea-
son was 1961 when he led NL in batting (.351),
named to Sporting News NL All-Star team, and
received the Gold Glove Award as outstanding

Clemente Tributes and Pictures on Six Inside Pages

Pittsburgh Post-Gazette

First Newspaper West of the Alleghenies

TUESDAY, JANUARY 2, 1973

Clemente Dies
In Plane Crash

'The Great One' Is Dead

Tragedy Evokes Tears,
Shock, Disbelief Here

sterilized severed stillborn sedition

war wombs

"They say they want a sample of my hair, a sample of my writing, and to subject myself to a line-up. Neither my hair nor my soul shall they have. I am free, and neither these bars nor this miserable and shameful country can keep me imprisoned."

— Marie Haydée Beltrán Torres

after the operación army ass-saulted mami
we sprang sterilized severed stillborn
sedition from stormed war wombs
screaming like lares lab rats
fugitive fetuses
fleeing fractured fallopian tubes
torn with rape razors
rusting rage between occupied taíno thighs
raided cervix invaded uterus
violated vaginas
conquered claimed
blue print battered battle bodies
brought forth from bondage
bandaged boricua by-product babies
breeding breathing barbed wire
bleeding bullets into contra-intercepted
captivity created colonial cavity coup
christian prison cells
constructed specially to quiet spic sisters
who shout out loud survival sounds
into aborted orphans' ears

kicked-out kon-verses

*"Remember them with kindness. It was not their choice to live
and die in the South Bronx."*

— Juan Bautista Castro

a prayer for
pre-historic pay more
or price-less last rights
slung from projects
swinging high b-side
the street lights
like in-fected rejects
kicked-out kon-verses write
alongside ancient adidas
and some ones un-done
air force ones overhanging
far above and beyond
broken glass theory gay-tor-AIDS
and way over the gutters
ground below the yellow snow
where barefootin' black babies
with heads hung under heaven
sporting lucky number seven jersey boys
reach up but just can't dunk
air jordans that got tossed
but still cost more than
the lay-up-and-a-way
or just a touch way too much
as they clutch de-flated
NBA ir-regulation basket-balls
against sunken hope chest
while the rest post-up posters
of madison square community
gardens where prison wardens
challenge shot-callers
or schoolyard b-ballers
done run one-on-one
against god's only son
while acid reign still drags
queens holding hail-mary king

james bible belts swingin' low like
thorny crown royalty
saviors-day sweat wet shit and dry spit
split dusted crust of just do it
fluids drown south bound subway
6 trains of thought slamming into half-smelly sewers
grown be-low black-top half court orders
where playas with jump start hearts
and pick and roll lost soles
sewn onto their swollen feet
sleep deep in an-other brothers
hand-me-down and out lifted spic knicks kicks

pair-a-dice cost

*"& so it is that I start this search confessing every ragged flag
I've praised & aim this pen to keep me true move me toward
creating definition."*

— Louis Reyes Rivera

puerto rico, not porto rico
i always made sure to say and write
the words clearly and rightly
in my best bad accent
an inner-city nuyorican approximation
declaration or a clearly stated or created
deafination of who i thought i was
puerto rico in english it means rich port
and in spanglish or maybe favela foreign
it be something like los miserables
like that play i never seen
in a language i couldn't hardly speak
least as far as i could remember
but i'd been there at least 365 times
awakened by supernatural sunlight and roosters
on a million different glossy mañanas
that were printed on one of those brooklyn bodega cheap
calendars your moms brought home as a $1 gift
for agreeing to agree to pay her unpaid bill next time
she came 'round to window thrift cop and shop
she put it up with a tiny rusted tack
in the hole that existed for that purpose
dead center in the kitchen directly above the sink
and right next to the porto rican ragged flag
that she got at the last pr day parade we ever went to
two years ago or a few years before that day
so now you couldn't hardly miss it at all ever
or when you went to get a glass of brown agua
or to wash your always dirty manos
she stared at it most days and i stared at it every day
imagined i was almost there transfixed by its unimaginable beauty
though i couldn't figure out if it was a copy of a real picture
or a copy of a painting of a real island or an illustration
of an illusion because the palm tree looked plastic

and the bluest water i'd ever seen looked unreal
like the blue eyes that i saw on a white man
on some television news show
or a picture i had seen of hawaii
that was a painting and not a picture
because hawaii didn't exist anymore either
but that calendar taught me to swim like a fish
and dive off the tallest cliffs like a smooth athlete
in red, white and blue speedos or commando
and i swear it gave me the darkest starkest tan
just like those old jíbaros from way over
in the albizu campos out in the sticks somewheres
where my grandfather i used to think must've came from
that my moms said were the color of the salt of the earth
that she regularly declared she would return to one day
or sooner than any of us would have expected
but i was already there writing poor pros poems
all about it all with cheap bics spics ink pen
that sometimes wouldn't write right or at all
that my mother got from the same bodega
where she got that crappy-ass calendar
while i was just splishing and a splashing
in a sea of verses and curses counting colors
on the backs of flying fish and other ufos
and catching clams between my jammed up toes
like my moms said my pops used to do back in the daze
when he was my age or just maybe a little bit older
and as i got older and started reading other things
besides "guzman's grocery, tenemos todo lo que tú necesitas"
i began spouting spit balls and mazel tov cock-tales
at all them white tourists who i now imagined in the picture
that might have been a painting hiding beneath the plastic
radio-active but still attractive palm of my hand trees
as they tainted the colores and screwed up the hues
and almost made me want to tear the calendar down
once or twice when moms wasn't always looking
and after my older sister once said it was "tacky" anyway
and i couldn't figure out if she meant the calendar
or probably that mythical place la isla del encounter
which caused my moms to smack sis upside the head
sigh and retreat to the living room alone by herself

to watch mexican or i think maybe venezuelan novelas
on our black and white tv that was imported from korea
via carlos on the corner right down the block and over
right next to guzman's bodega where they had everything
a nuyorican could possibly never ever need ever at all
or even when you ain't really know it not at first

caribbean see/sí

"& the erosion of polluted waters will dissolve me in slow motion agony."

— Tato Laviera

diving head first out of your drunken boat
i'm drowning in your slave-ship sewage
a bleeding carib head sub-merged
six feet deep under shit level
buoyed by garbage
floating in waste products
sucking contamination
suckling radiation
between blistered lips
while snorting whore institutions
pollutions
through the burning nostrils
of the indigenous hostiles
gasping
gurgling
guzzling
gasoline
drenched pipe dreams
that feel like the taíno
drenched in drano
and tastes like comet
or the victor's vomit
and stinks like your loco-motive
breath stench of ara-whack death
but it's either swim or sink
or drown or drink
and my cup runs over-bored

crossing 110th street

"It's just a moment, we die every night."

— William Carlos Williams

the flowers they sent were already dead
because they went to the wrong address
because every corner had a funeral parlor
right next to a liquor store
right next to the flower shop
where the clerk wrote down the wrong address
because he was drunker than the driver
who mowed down the careless kid
crossing across 110th street
past the liquor store
that was right next to the funeral parlor
where his mother was waiting
for her freshly dead flowers

The careless kid

crossing across 110th st

past the liquor store

that was right next to

the funeral parlor

private property

"Not one damn brick belongs to me, not one damn block."

—Miguel Piñero

Porto Rican housing project
Buffed then abandoned
boricua buildin
missing foundation
with no walls and windows
or rufo or floors
and one busted door
needing a graffitied key
that almost opens up
only from the other side
ways to no exit here
or there be nothing
worth some thing
just the residues and don'ts
of un-able-to-be-paid dues
and already swiped pipes,
pilfered plumbing,
and a broken window
theories of racial spatial
de-concentration
anything of value
violated and ravaged
savaged by scavengers
assaulted by arsonists
pilfered property or more
or less raped real estate
left for theft kept and slept
on warehoused whorehouses
abandoned random sore spot
rotting squats condemned
carcasses of a foreclosed
future shock

still I stay in the way
neither there nor anywhere
this un-raveling autonomous
re-zoned anti-treaty black list

pissed on terrorist slit wrist
who don't own my own
broken and entered home
land of lead paint (in)stead
I wait for the knock at midnight
and I listen closely
for the sounds
of landlords
with re-leases
lawyers
with master-locks
and cops
with fiction eviction
notices posted along with
neo-nooses and closed borders
colonial court orders
and institution constitutions
know your rights
and all wrongs

i know they are coming soon
to a shelter near me
and although they say
i am worth-less
they still want all
i am worth
i cost nothing for now
but i am not free
and i am not mine
be-cause mi casa
no es mía
and today
i am still
someone else's
private property
falling apart at the...

¡pero coño!
now
mi casa
es
tu condo!

sex and the streets
(a love poem para mi barrio)

"Your buildings are burning up, that we got to stop."

— Bimbo Rivas

la calle-jera climbs up
and out and over
on top broken-glass
ceilings keeping it
reeling bleeding
rubber bullets
over el barrio
flowing buckets
that paint the town
red-scarlet letter
sticky flow throw ups
spraying swaying
sky high above
housing projects
showing off to all
her smooth rooftop
mad love move-ments
illicit amor well after midnight
shadow flash dancing to some
sexed up salsa slut strut
blasting from out a stolen stereo
she sing-shouts along a loud
then adds some improvised
lies and ribald ballads
to the enamored full moon
that nearly blushes
but still hollas back on track
if not quite as brash smashed
boldly she tosses off and away
her man-made manacles
shell-toe shackles
barbed-wire bodice
concertina clothes
and policed panties
and sends them sailing

down deep into the art-less
alleyway and bash-full
man-holes far below her full
metal fantasies and stands
alone accused seething
and deeply breathing
these ill-legal tender kneads
no longer even needing
to plead or please anyone
tonight she be truly freed
the shimmying seductress
begins her dance frantically
deep inside the black-out night
as ill-legalized security sirens
screech squawk shit talk
all along the chastity avenues
way down around uptown
below where the bare-breasted
barrio ballerina pops and un-locks
lust thrust back smack and forth
in circular coda loca-motions
as her slum lovers serenade
sing her shameless name in vain
and all the other abandoned
branded buildings surrounding
begin to make similar sound tracks
to her screaming teeming theme
as they will smolder and smoke
and finally forcefully fiercely fearlessly
the condemned cat-callers all catch (a) fire

just a stones throw
from the wall of silence
and 69's violence
when village idiots
in badges and blue

GAY PROHIBITION G
CORUPT$ COP$
FEED $ MAFIA

STOP ATTACKS
ON LESBIANS & GAY

squared off against
street stars

tran-sister (Feb 19, 2002)

"Hell hath no fury like a drag queen scorned."

— Sylvia Rivera

twisted slit wristed
suicide lipstick
lay away lady
with rainbow painted radio
left leaning antenna
left of the dial
battered and bashed
past outcast
harassed and healed
as you kneeled
on the back of a bumper
bearing a slick glitter sticker
saying the bitch is back
to back static between station
to station saint vincent's
soul salvation sound
and fury freezing
on any unnamed avenues
and unspoken sidewalks
just a stone's throw
from the wall of silence
and '69's violence
when village idiots
in badges and blue
squared off against street stars
in stilettos and scars
and a spic scorned and re-born
as a drag queen rosa parks
started a riot that sparked
a rebelution

how do i love thee?

"now I awake to find that the underneath of your beautiful poetry pamphleteering against the mob of stars took me nowhere."

—Tato Laviera

how do i love thee
let me count the daze
i marched down wall street
fist in the air and heart in my throat
while bashing down barricades
and occupying everything!
i faced the pepper spray
with nothing but a red bandana
that smelled like you...
i shouted
"free mumia"
and/or "maroon!"
at the top of my lungs
and screamed
"free puerto rico!"
"and/or palestine!"
'til i was hoarse
or worse better
and chanted
rally 'round the red, gold, black and green!
and believed we would
and wailed
smash the state and/or eat the rich!
and thought we could
i devoured the che guevara book on guerilla warfare
that you bought for my birthday twice
and even the ten or more noam chomsky and howard zinn books
that you said i simply had to (try to) read...
and recited every word
of public enemy's fight the power
to you like it was poetry
i set fire to the nike town in midtown
and stayed to fan the flames
i threw a brick through the disney store

on 125th street and amster-damn avenue
and hit mickey mouse dead in the head
i wheatpasted eat the rich posters
on the new luxury highrise condo
on malcolm x blvd and almost got arrested
and bombed the brand spanking newly built
pharmaceutical company in the barrio
because you said it made you sick
i slapped the mayor straight in his face
just cuz i knew you wanted me to
and i shot the sheriff and the deputy
and the nypd police chief too...
and ran up in the house of congress
guns blazing with nothing but four bullets
a ragged anarchist black flag
and a soiled picture of you
in my cargo pocket...
i assassinated the president
of someone else's united states
and lived to tell why...
i threatened the vice-president,
secretary of state, and the first lady too
though i didn't really know why
i wrote you line upon line
of lucid love letters and pleas, please, please...
while waiting patiently on lockdown
and read right between the lines
of every pittance political pamphlet or paltry prose poem
that you ain't never ever wrote back....

for Julia (Jul 6, 1953)

"I have found myself, upon finding my verse."

— Julia de Burgos

poetry sweet as sugar cane
sharp as the migrant's machete
cutting away distances
between the statue's sadness
and the master's madness
mixing cold pale with pure coal black
ink and hair of kink beauty queen
with full lips and swaying hips
stolen by the white king's cold grip
searing dark flesh sinking drinking
into clear caribbean water
turned to wine
to battle invincible currents
and escape the grasp
of their slave ships
rising once more from below
naked as nature
free as the sea and alive as art
with sacred bleeding heart still beating
to begin a new awakening
with your beloved body
un-broken and forever bronzed

poetry
sweet
as
sugar
cane

sharp
as
the
migrant's

machete

cutting away distances

love is revolution
(a poem/prayer for Che María)

"Part of being a revolutionary is creating a vision that is more humane. That is more fun too. That is more loving. It's really working to create something beautiful."

—Assata Shakur

born in the bottom of sodom
a broken slingshot
dropped in the rot and forgot
blessed as a have not
beat by the street bittersweet
love isn't lost just damaged
and damned in defeat
my sweet beloved cost
slum seeds sacrificed
for once i thought twice
roll of the dice in this life
we all pay the price
of warfare or welfare
ashamed we bare the
nameless daughter
or slaughter abort her
or play the game
berated ill-fated
too right or left
to die still born
un-adorned
with a thorn
inside a side
entombed
in the womb
consumed
while still
in bloom...

so follow assata i said
in recollection
ghetto or god will provide
you with protection

but outside
children dying
politicians lying
cut throat corporations
gangland generations
x and king forgotten
huey newton shot and
arms and evolution
love is revolution...

torn from the horror of harlem
hell or a hard-knock life
rife with strife a pocket knife
packed in-side a master-lock
war at your door for-ever sure
that barely a stone's throw
jesus will cheat us or lead us
straight out of death row
prisons and schisms
and slums and beating
hearts and the starving
arts and marching armies
of another armegeddon
in the midst of being born
battered behind prison walls
or just scrawled on project
halls of injustice and no truth
for the "young black youth"
so they turn bullet proof
but still the bombs be
bursting see babylon
burning still yearning
living and un-learning
in schoolyards where we
fool-bards flash zip guns
while living low on funds
this won't be much fun
but a baby just maybe
this one's a second first
chance a fleeting glance

a cheating romance
or our final first dance...

so follow assata i said
a resurrection
ghetto or god will abide
a new direction

but outside
youth uprising
old men criticizing
police in position
radical religion
confrontation camps
dead flowers for fred hampton
but armed with resolution
love is revolution

so follow assata
i say
follow assata
i say
follow assata
i pray

cara cuerpo y corazón
en la cuna de babylon
el amor es un conspiración
y tú y yo revolución...

brown boy (for Zion Indio)

"here you were: to be loved. To be loved, baby, hard, at once,
and forever, to strengthen you against the loveless world."

—James Baldwin

…and then here
you were born
from real(idad) love
into and against
a love-less world
a jíbaros sinewy arms
a masai marathoners legs
ten inquisitive little fingers
diez wandering tiny toes
a kinky brown sugar crown
amor de rey
forever feeling free
rainbow skinned
with a heavenly halo
floating bronzed above
and 'round irradiant
indio face of reality
re-vealed zion(!)
had came up-on us
opened-wide with this
child wisdom with no tears
staring back at me
neither more nor less
than the rebel face of god(!)
and the/your future(!)

but i cried aghast(!)
seeing only ugly visions
unchained and unhinged
of a love-less world
full from the crushed
cruz of these fictions
black earth burning
scorched flesh bitches
brewed and screwed

whip-cracking overseers
inside a hot box death camps
bullet proof backpacks
hooked on lynching
trees with strange fruits
hanging around killing
fields where today there
be peewee league prison
cells and central casting
dirty needle inna-city
cemetery sanctuaries
in side genocidal ghetto
gulags where the only
african gods left were
all already stopped
and frisked
and found
guilty...

my earth-colored brown boy
you was pristine perfection
powerful! beyond a dream
in spite of a nightmare
the future unfolding
beauty untold and
unmatched

but my thoughts was
beaten blind-sided
and bombed
and my memory was/is
dis-figured damaged
dumb-founded
making all of this
hit and missed
his-story hideous....

poem for San Miguelito (Jun 16, 1988)

"dreamt I was a poet & writin' silver sailing songs."

—Miguel Piñero

genesis
of
blood
and
piss
sick
slit
wrist
and
bruce
lee
kicks
shopping
list
pharmacist
nickel
bag
nihilist
addict
alchemist
revelation
realist
tecato
terrorist
waving
a
porto
rican
power
fist
at
hit
or
missed
last
good
night
judas
kissed

the junkie christ

"When a poet dies a whole community is affected."

—Miguel Algarín

junkie
jesus
genocide
preacher
pusher
porto
rican
pride
locked
inside
slum
suicide
lived
and
died
as
a
ghetto
slide
gypsy
cab
ride
to
the
low
east
side
where
you
can
glide
but
you
can't
not
hide

last call (Mar 3, 2004)
a poem written for Papoleto and his memories

"if you don't become a missing person every now and then you will never know who the hell you are."

—Pedro Pietri

El Reverendo Pedro
claimed
agent orange
first painted his future black
sometime around 1898
or 1944
or 1947
or 1967
or the day before today
which was yesterday
or maybe the day after
tomorrow
during the first to last draft
in the beginning of the end
of a nuyorican nightmare
where roosevelt's roughriders
in hang 'em high gliders
first began to drop 'nam bombs
from tio sam's sticky hands
onto a sickly spic soldier's shoulders
40,000 feet above unholy hell
or texas and too far from his homeboy's
hormigueros hideout
or the satanic his-panic hospital
in the bronx or lebanon
where he had no health-nobody-care
insurance to pay his way
and was scorned and informed
before being not quite mourned
by storm troopers in scrubs
that his cultural credit card compra
couldn't cure his cancer
that day or any day
and he was gonna die soon enough

any ol' way anyway
and if he wanted to try to pay
on the porto rican poetry lay away
they would need something in writing
yesterday the other day and everyday
even on the holy sun-day
with an all glory signatory
of jesucristo hisself
or some other non-nuyorican
person of state-us
and undue other-word-ly
wealth or good health
so the black on black
on both sides sick spic
spirit soon succumbed
and eventually did died
from a systemic spanglish
suicide outside the inside
of the outside of the low east side
and in due time and again
began to haunt the shit-stained
cemetery streets of the loisaida
like a living dead deceased
poetic priest graveyard bard
for the societally scarred
and eventually even re-wrote
his own re-evolving door
first, second and last outcast obituary
as an after-word for all to re-read
in invisible indivisible ink
printed on an unpaid traffic ticket
on the first page after the last page
en la pig latin dispensable prensa
and on the side of a dis-re-guarded
re-incarnated carnation milk carton
condemned casita next to an ad
looking for a cure for a lost nationality
in-fected reality nuyorican malady
that was crammed inside the outside
of an overflowing hobo's garbage can
made in japan and left beside inside

a phone booth that was out of service
and didn't never accept long distance
collect calls from porto ricano
political prisoners in any way anyway
but did had a recently re-re-corded
broken English message from mexico
for all to play yesterday or later that day
or any other day during the day
that said, to be read out loud:
> One is still a crowd...
> except when there are two
> or less

con los santos no se juega

"y echar brujos de fufú y espíritus malos a los que nos tratan
como naborias y exclavos."

—Tato Laviera

sticky city summers
we would melt
into the concrete jungle
bantu brown and black,
brothers boricuas
brandishing barrio
batás bongós
djembes congas
cocolos shit talkin'
joke crackin' banging
on garbage cans
and graffitti drenched
benches beating back
babylon and the sirens blare
with sweet spiritual sounds
worthy of obatalá, yemayá,
and mi mamá
magic mixed with memories
of alkebulan over oceans, oshun,
ogun minus the chains
on our legs and shackles
on our crown-less heads
no radios violating the vibe
zulu zen to zion
ghetto soweto to god damn,
man no tell-a-visions
that we couldn't tell ourselves
'cept a stolen zenith
owned by liberation loan
plugged into a free zone,
then smashed against the asphalt
when 'macho lost in seven
fuck, so close to heaven
we coulda lost ourselves
but we found what we weren't looking for

by a patch of dead grass that
wouldn't have even filled a nickel bag in '82
but me and you were already the most natural high
no lie, do or die was the cancer
but you and I found another answer
rapped tighter than lamb's bread
and we smoked with fire in our fingertips
spics, shanty santos spitting ron rico
into open wounds while worshiping warrior's wombs
while we cooked culture and made medicinal música,
melodies llamando, llamando, llamando a afrika
riddims that uprise and sound designed
to blow the white man's mind and it was all mine,
and yours, because I was we and I was I
and I was looking for the perfect beat down
crack calles that called me nigga
until I found something bigga
in a botánica that dispensed bombas and plans
guns and helping hand-in-hands
and we made our last stand on the corners
of the corners of crack houses and calle churches
ellegua bembe, barrio, baby benin blessed buddhas
Rising high like spirits sealed in slum sparrows
with busted wings and rusted arrows
and not a prayer to be bought
but we was already almost caught right there
mounted and moaning dancing and dangerous
like a double-edged ax with chango strapped to our backs
nearly there, oh yeah, oya, aha, ellegua!!!....
'til some cracker called the culture cops
to cart our orishas away
but by then we were long gone...
ache

wrought warrior (maferefun ogun)

"who's the one who spits on tools…"

— Jayne Cortez

the scrap-yard thief
with hardware teeth
and hacksaw lockjaw
carved ratchet raw
used his crow-bar scars
to cut thru chromium bars
and his shrapnel spit
like a brass-knuckle drill bit
with his third-rail nails
he hammered his way out of jails
and beat plowshares into swords
to wage bolt-cutter wars
with metal-passage machete
tensile blade at the ready
and his nigga-wrench mouth
steel-wool scourge north to south
a man-dingo unchained
or metal malcolm makin' it plain
with titanium tongue
and dead-bolt cult gun
he aimed his black alloy rod
to turn iron-man into (a) God

pero
tu
sabes
que
para
tu gente
you
was
always
el cantante

tu gente

"He was a barrio Poet. He had the message of the street kids."

— Larry Harlow

To
them
you
was
just
another
of
them
suffering
spic
singers
pero
tu
sabes
que
para
tú
gente
you
was
always
el
cantante
de
los
cantantes
coquí
de
los
callejeros
sabio
of
calle
sol
jíbarito
del

ghetto
grito
sonero
de
los
santos
todopoderoso
para
los
pobrecitos
pastor
para
los
sin
voz
y
la
lengua
de
nuestra
liberacíon

steppin' into beauty (June 6, 2006)

"In my music, you can hear the Latin elements, because when you're playing jazz, you can only play what you are."

— Hilton Ruiz

salsa steppin' side by side
with a tp strut and stride
outside an old new orleans dive
so far from the manhattan mambo
música land of enchantment
called the boogie woogie bronx
where eight-year-old island eyes
first met mingus and mined mary lou
dug deeper into the duke
hailed hubbard and henderson
studied with sanders
played with paquito
prayed with palmieri
and practiced 'til you was ready
to roll with rashan roland
and jam with jackie and giovani
on latin jazz blast and bomba blues
built to last by birdland hands
by way of the motherland
and dropped out of hand
onto the wrong bandstand
when you took a wrong step
too far out of boricua be-bopper
bounds into bourbon street bar
utopia and backed away
back into a final show of force
played by police pedestrians
with batons or blackjacks
or some other non-musical
blunt instruments
that were instrumental
in fracturing your face
cracking your skull

and inducing a concert
closed-file
post katrina coma
that killed you while en camino
to composing another New York story

...su final (June 29, 1993)

"Death will be late to bring us aid."

— William Carlos Williams

El periódico de ayer
read that el fin
día de tu suerte
finally struck back
tomorrow morning
from too long mourning
your seven long times away
from la Che Che Cole

don't call me nigger, whitey!
(a slave for life)

"A wealthy man here had a boy named Reuben, almost white, whom he caused to be branded in the face with the words; 'A slave for life.'"

—St. Louis Gazette (6th Nov. 1845)

no white man ever called me "nigger"
at least not to my face to face
but I've been told that I was once called "cargo"
by conquistadors
as I sailed across the middle passage
shackled and suffocating
side by side sick on a stinking ship
with hundreds of other abducted Africans
on our way to another america
where I can nearly remember
when I was branded a "captive"
by their captain and traded
by my abductors for rum and guns
and then scarred, tarred and separated
from my home and my own
and infected, inspected and sold
on the grab and go auction block
to the highest bidders or buyers
and I do recollect when I was named "property"
by the overseers who trapped and trained me
on how to be a good house "slave for life"
a label from cradle to grave
by breaking my legs, severing my fingers
slitting my tongue and selling my one son
and I ain't ever forgot when I was renamed "Negro"
by the owner who thought
that 400 years of 200 lashes on my black and burning back
had tamed me from trying to flee the misery of the massa's
gold mines, sugar mills and cotton fields
or when they said I was "contraband"
as I donned a yanquís uniform to fight for my freedom
during their uncivil war
and "strange fruit"

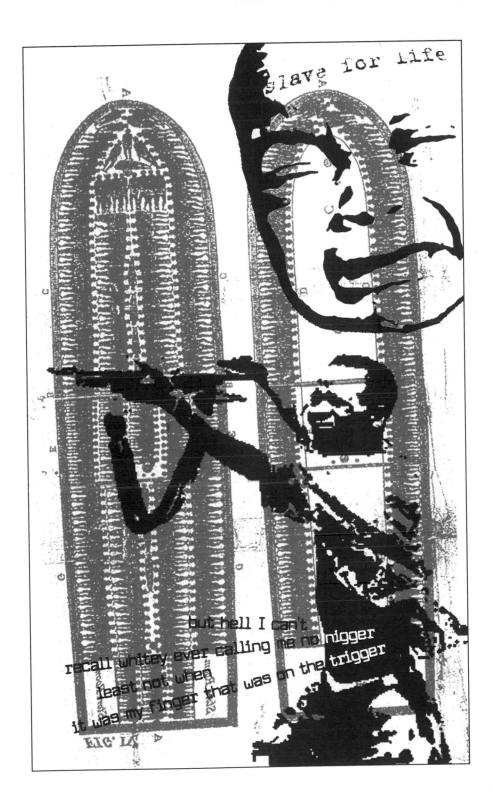

when I was hunted and hung from a southern tree
for fighting for my own civil rights
and then mandated "separate but equal"
and taught how to be "three tenths of a man" in they schools
and I won't soon forget when I was beaten, burned
and nearly broken to make way for a better "servant"
and "token" "colored" man and then colored as a "convict"
and a "criminal" and a "culprit" in their torture tombs and death row cells
where the white man's heaven is still the black man's hell
but hell I can't recall whitey ever calling me no "nigger"
least not when it was my finger that was on the trigger

revolution re-runs

the revolution
will not be played pimped or punk'd
niggas should know this

the revolution
can not be commercialized
if you keep it real

manmade © (Aug 12, 1988)

"every line means something"

— Jean-Michel Basquiat

sweatshop basquiat
auctioned on the chopping block
get your copy now

Black bodies for sale
man-made and man-u-fractured
Get em while they shot

Do not hesitate
This offer won't cum again
So buy black right now!

Do we have a bid?
On this one prime specimen
Comes complete with chains

Guaranteed to slave
From the cradle to the grave
Or your money back

And if it be dead
He may be worth twice as much
As he was a live

niggaz anonymous 12-step program

"damn/if I ain't known Niggers I ain't ever smelled shit."

—Jesús Papoleto Meléndez

first they came for the outlawz
and I said I was legit
then they came for the vandalz
and I said that I had quit
then they came for the felonz
and I didn't give a shit
then they came for the junkiez
and I said I weren't one
then they came for the hookerz
and I said I knew of some
then they came for the hustlerz
though we thought they'd never come
then they came for the broken
but I didn't need a fix
so they asked for the outspoken
and I blended in the mix
then they asked me for a token
and I led them to some spicz
so they went to find the homeless
and I showed them to the door
and when they asked to see the hopeless
I just said I wasn't poor
and when they came to get the niggaz
I replied I weren't no more

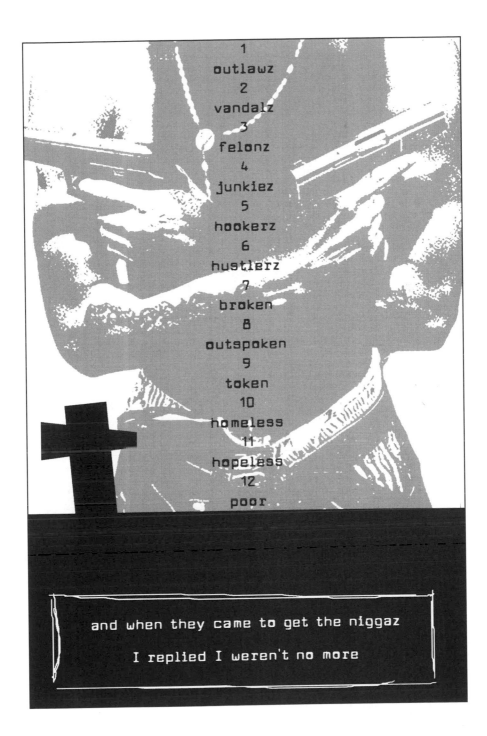

resistance 101

"And today I celebrate, my first cry, also my great shout, is in its beginnings."

—Lolita Lebrón

the raw reality of rican resistance

is the taino/the yoruba/the jíbaro

slaves/santos/seditionaries

subversives/screams

suffering/sacrifice

survival

spanish boots

on boricua bodies

indigenous up-risings

esclavo conspiracies

broken window theories

abolitionist actions

shackled africans

betances/bracetti

sewing the seeds

of rebelation/resistance

reservations/desecrations

el grito de lares

voices 'lifted like pal mares"

and the nation-less nation

state of con-fusion/ill-lusion

of borinqueños burning sugarcane

spain/shame

remember the maine

acid reign/nothing to be gained

here/there/their

and no where/wear

for art thou

now brown cow

bow and scrape

re-shape/rape

and pillage

burn the village

till the soil/toil/boil/broil

until fully cooked/rooked/shook

one star and bars

and cages/en-rages

center stages/minimum wages

seekin' Puerto Rican Pack mules

fools/golden rules

they schools/tools

teachin'/preachin'

beseechin'/reachin'

for the past

last of the po'ricans

freakin'/weakin'/beacon light

white knight/night/wrong is re-write

his-stories told/bought and re-sold

old fairy tales

third rails

pass is fails

prisons and jails

hail mary's

load to carry

like lola y la borinqueña

brandishing bullets/bibles

bootstraps/bad raps/traps

and the porto rico ponce massacre

hiram/elias

and riggs and rigged

elections/injections
rejections/connections
canales realidades
jailed in jayuya
for the heinous crime
of a re-defined puerto rican state
(of mind)
less pushers/pirates/presidents
and the ponce plaza prophets
campos y corretjer y coraje,
y imprisonment for insurrection
instigation/infiltration,
separation/demilitarization
sterilization/marginalization
indignation/imagination
and independence is resistance/insistence
and rebellion y revolutionary
violence/silence
sit-ins/dark skins
marín and the marines
social scenes/seens
death and docility be damned
jammed/crammed/on the lambs
griselio and oscar
and an attempted assassination
of someone else's united nation
lolita and rafa, and irvin, and andrés
y más de veinte y cinco años
for an arm-in-arm with arms
assault on the capitalist
common wealth
congress/colonizer's
despisers/proselytizers

rage/resistance

ríos and rivera

and detonations/demonstrations

inundations/cast-strations

downpression god damned

rammed like sardine canned

by landlords/community boreds

hospital wards/young lords

takin it to the streets is watching

latin kings with cross over dreams

on lock down/sacred ground/hell bound

el barrio/barcelló/roselló

y qué se yo/nuevo yo

jíbaritos/jitterbugging jesus

on the corners of the corners

of the calles de nuyo-rican/freakin

still seekin a cause/or just be-cause

in these (un)united states

urban warfare/guerrilla welfare

ghetto workfare/un-fair

food stamps/concentration camps

fuel for thought/caught/taught

salsa con sabotage sold and bought

puerto rican peoples armies

of angry apostles/fossils

and autonomous military macheteros

messiahs/pariahs/wanna take you high-a'

national liberation/frustration/re-creation

of one nation under (african) gods

under-ground/under represented/resented

prevented/lamented/re-invented

inducted/instructed/ricanstructed

lucy and luis

and alicia and adolfo

and alejandrina and antonio

and carlos and carmen

and ricardo and elizam

and dylcia and juan

and edwin and haydee

and no solace for solis

and Avelino

and Filiberto!!!

que viva el MACHETERO!!!

and MIRA/CAL/FALN again

and again(st)/rising rents

fbi and I against i and i

and i for an i

love and liberated zoncs

and sticks and stones

and broken homes

and skulls and bones

and bombs/psalms/uncle toms

cancer/cures/criollo

camp david save it

and goliath defy us

but don't dare try us

and victims

and vieques

and vultures

and vampires

and violence

and value

and victory

and what Don Pedro

once called valor...

prisoners of colonialism

"The very ink with which history is written is merely fluid prejudice"

—Mark Twain

puerto rico
is an island but
it is not "i" land
it was taken away long ago
stolen by
conquistadors and colonizers
police and thieves
sailors and soldiers
who aimed
ideology arms
at open land mines
of freedom
with laws and locks
contracts and chains
treaties and terrorism

they tossed our jibaro keys
into freshly subjugated seas
and gnawed holes
in our canoes
and cracked our sensitive skulls
with sticks and schools

they placed barbed wire
across slit veins
and built military reservations
on naked earth

they painted prisons
on the landscapes of our flesh
drew temporary lines
in white sand
and permanent scars
on brown skin
and drafted maps to show us

prisoners of colonialism

and
once
we
learned
to
forget,
they
stamped
our
memories

PUERTO RICO
US PROPERTY

the nature of our captivity
and the state
of their control

they burned albizu's body
at the stake
and planted
amerikan flags
in his raw wounds

they misspelled history
renamed us
prisoners of colonialism
and once we learned to forget
they stamped our memories
"u.s. property"

august 1, 2010

lolita lebrón
said she did not come to kill
but to die for us

lolita once said
men won't free puerto rico
so we women will

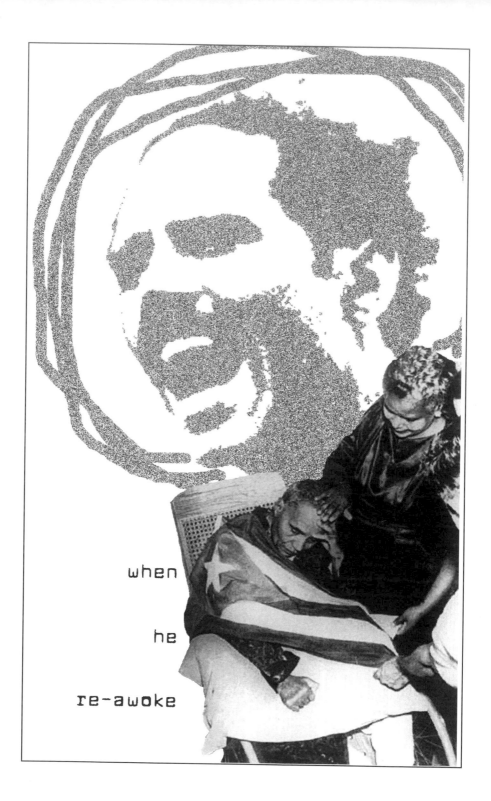

when

he

re-awoke

april 21, 1965

albizu's carcass
still smelled of radiation
when he re-awoke

pedro's got a bomb
set for the fourth of july
and his fuse is short

september 23, 2005

filiberto's dead!
this could be the first trumpet
or maybe the last

el commandante
had nothing to be gained here
so he died for us

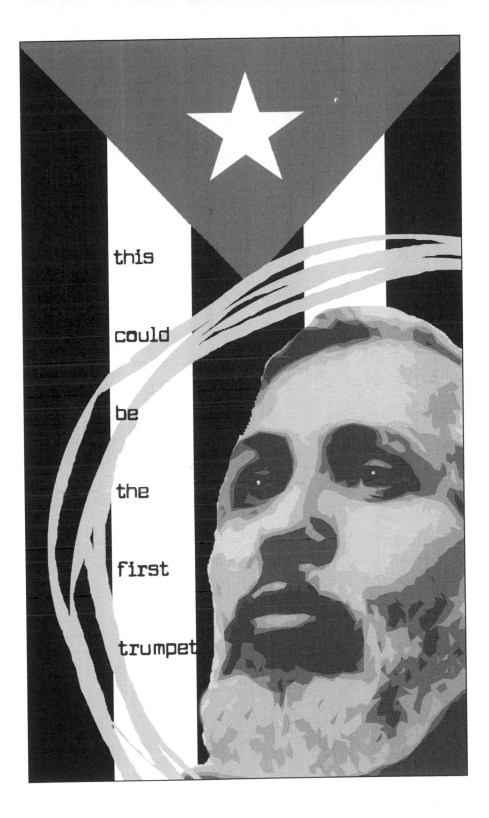

bombs over el barrio
(front-line free-style)

"This is a war that's been going on since the invasion of North America."

— Pedro Pietri

bombs over body bag-dad or borinquen
el barrio bathed in an rotc raytheon
radioactive rio sumpul
combat contra cultural
revolution constitution
pollution retribution
glow gung-ho ghetto gulf grenada
invaders instigators darth vaders
now is laters al-qaedas go raiders
land takers and LA lakers
wheelers and dealers
and super bold stealers
feeling spoils of war or blood for oil
dead youth proof yankee truth
injust-us and the school of the american
way decay yesterday is today's
nepalm nagasaki news report
sports forts fighting for the american
dream team cream m16 another nazi scheme
seen syria sandinista soldier spic ku klux klan
hiroshima hole-accost hand to hand in the sudan
panamanian strong man death don't give a damn
who i am mother fodder daughter dollar
make me wanna holler
desert storm before the calm
say adiós to dad and mom
because whatever can will go wrong
it's survival of the strong
so you better drop the bomb
on uncle psalm and uncle tom
'cause vieques equals one, two, three vietnam(s)...

VS

nigga, bitch, faggot
slain with one slip of the tongue
from a verbal gun

wetback, spic, beaner
shot dead with a word weapon
becomes poetry

nuyorican rulez

"I made up a language in which to exist."

—Elizabeth Alexander

english is broken hear
just like they rulez
nigga wrenched
racked ritmos
reality wrecked
and left in ruins
strewn across
stolen spaces
and parceled places
sneaking passed
porto ricos past
into nuevo yos
of stinking subway
six trains of thought
stuck between
swiped syllables
spoken in imperfect
sign slanguages
sinking six degrees
separated by sugar
coca-cain and dis-abled
streets and sewer streams
of un-consciousness
bracing on beyond the spacing
of two-spirited split tongues
wrung and swung
on dirty laundry lines
off fire no escapes
hung from broken
boogaloo bootstraps
boosted from barrio bodegas
snatched back to back
or branded and abandoned
in burned out Boricua
building blocs and his-panic
attack hiphop houses

where
agüeybaná
first met
obatalá

y los de aquí
said welcoming
to los de allá

Grand St

Graham Av-Av de Puerto Rico

BIKE LANE

PORTO RICO

WE ACCEPT
FOOD
STAMPS
EBT

of the unholy ojalá heroin
nod to the african gods
inside seventies soulsa
stop and cop
stupor mercados
asimilados
against fenced in
four letter mis-spelled words
and as-matic add-verbs
sprung unsung
from cultural cages
rican rages porto rock pages
written in indivisible ink
stains over tortured tecatos
and tattooed manteca men
backed smack against chalk
lines on crack pavements
atop affordable portable housing
project palm of your hand
trees outside prison food stamp
deconcentration summer camps
where busted radiator rhymes
and multicultural minds
grind against petty crimes
swaying me from sea to shining
can you see them dancing
free mambo mouth to mouth
from way up north and back
to back all the way down south
where agüeybaná first met obatalá
y los de aquí said welcoming
to los de allá

sketching schematics

"Turn off the stereo this country gave you, it is out of order."

—Pedro Pietri

scratching at the signs of the surface
a working wage is worth the weight of the worth-less
south Bronx is tribal survival
one micro-phone versus gideon's bible
rivals war hardcore only to be
gunned down sounds like cultural casualty
but black is black until hijacked into the abstract
and fiction becomes fact
when your world is under attack
ghetto streams the microphone fiends
still tryna snatch the cream
of this penitentiary pipe dream
rhyme addicts sketching schematics
on the edge of panic with a semi-automatic
but shit's hard when you're slum scarred
dis-regard or draw a bad card
calling out the national guard
on the third ward praise the lord
billboards hanging from a short chord
strange fruit rob and loot ill-repute
law suits jacking with a jack boot
you shoot and I shoot
but it don't compute
square roots cut down at the roots
but these daze you are what you says
so watch what you plays
mister DJs....

cain and abel is an aesop's fable
the king of rock got a record label
planet rock and you don't stop
so take your best shot
got biggie or tupac?
cuz ain't no telling who gonna hate cha
when it's done by the forces of nature
and ain't nobody left that can reach ya
when you're paid in full

or a poor righteous teacher
but it's strictly bizness
still you say what is this?
and you say what is this?
then you say what is this?...

so you keep
scratching at the signs of the surface
a world away from the Gods and the earth is
south bronx dissonant resistance
one microphone is still ill-legal bizness
is this war what for all eyes on me
get free from the jealous one's envy
mountain top beat bop until the bombs drop
born one block from a shell shocked
scott la rock battle zone slum al capone
on ya motorola phone
all alone in the terrordome
still-matic ciphering static
pass the hand grenade
and my adidas from the attic
cuz shit's real black steel
make a deal
be real to feel the mass appeal
hard times hard lines
drop a rhyme
criminal minds
standing on a landmine
hiphop's sweat shops
forget me knots
and the have nots
and what cha gots?
real G's
wounded knees
little seize
cop a please

cuz these daze
you are what you say
and who you betray
jam master j
let us pray...

rap sheets (last writes)

"words are loaded pistols"

— Jean-Paul Sartre

sweet charlotte street concrete rip rap sheets
recycled bambaataa beats suites
and banana boat grace note quotes
wrote with raw throats
beneath bronx barretto
boogaloo bombas dropping,
popping ain't no stopping
under uprooted polluted air
air wear supply skies scarred
dis-bards and nerve center
break and enter dissenter
mentors with vinyl spinal chord
young lord cross-color swords
sling section eights a day too late
diggin in the crates for vice-roy
or James brown to get up and git git down
as unbound burned to the ground b-boy black
brown bodies drowned in a last poets loco-motion
oceans in time behind enemy (subway) line
scofflaw fines or mock rock steady
petty crimes and "no po' ricans or dogs allowed"
mis-spelled street signs of the furious fire last times
felonious funk shit spit and writ like julio 204
or shafts big score above can't afford 'em roads
and below barrio bar code overloads
where mr. charlie chase mis-spent dead presidents
into congressional confessional booths
where they float or vote between curtis mind-fields
and raw deals stealing samples like ex vandals
from soup kitchen snitches crashing like charles bronson
billie jack johnsons upon cold crushed brothers
savage skulls shaking stray spray can stick it to the man
x-clan pot shots at cops from ran-dumb roof tops
carrying sub-mean machine cultures
on each whipper whip hip through abandoned strip malls
a-cross no cost lost on the bronx express

way to your (h)art attack cold fact racking
up-rising bombers brandishing blasting fania fat cap rap
strapped around downtown no salary shooting galleries
sellin' us back our basquiat black snatched off slices
of piece, love and ruby dee for a nominal fee
LEE in just be-gun hill shoot to kill gil scott heroin
housing projects In addicted un-restricted
and un-sound playgrounds and terrible tenement
remnants of a notorious nation
under a disapproved groove
300,000 ona move like the mighty force moses
told us with ray guns aimed at the rockin' remnants
of riots reaching the (hunts) point of no return
burn baby burning block after block
(busting) boom box beat downs of stolen sound
views and the daily blues on sacred grounds
that we called the boogie down
or somewhere down 'round about uptown
saturday night before vinyl's final fight
and CDs Mp3 free flight
on sunday bloody sunday morning
dis-owning the preachers' last warning
while our teachers were still mourning
the evidence of the evident
death of hiphop

krylon koltrane

"I cross out words so you will see them more."

I was raised in the ghetto
watching it burn like nero
smoking imitation indo
looking for an anti-hero
maybe Miguel Piñero
or some man-made pendejo
or just robert's dinero
pero that added up to cero
so I crawled on caterwauls
body sprawled on bathroom stalls
even scrawled in project halls
cuz I sucked at basketball
but I slam dunked overhauls
on pristine suburban malls
writing rhymes of rise and falls
on the sides of chinese walls
and the backs of billboards
owned by liquor stores and whores
cutting umbilical chords
with a subliminal sword
and the slanguage I could hoard
cuz it's all I could afford
but in short I got bored
of my inner-city tour
so I painted crude collisions
on the wings of carrier pigeons
and re-wrote my inner visions
on the insides of incisions
but they buffed off my transmissions
and deciphered long divisions
so I made my indecision
to compose without permission
spraying stains on blue trains
like a krylon koltrane
with an aerosol aim
at the city's remains

like

a

krylon

koltrane

with

an

aerosol

aim

came my cut-rate acclaim
and my fame in the game
from a burn to a flame
for an untitled name so
I climbed on a rhyme
like the franz kline of mime
hanging pieces of my mind
from a cryptic clotheline
and in time I got signed
by the top turpentine
for a half-done design
of a copy written crime
hanging in a mausoleum
by a pile of rustoleum
posting posters on per diem
at a fisher price premium
for a tourist consortium
in the roman coliseum
so I tried my best to free em
from this methadone museum
and I took what I defaced
and replaced what they erased
and threw back what I misplaced
in the wreckage and the waste
of my taste of inner space
but there was no refuge place
from my final fall from grace
so I left without a trace

write on

"Everything flows, nothing stands still"

— Heraclitus

250 million dollars
to snuff street scholars
from 73 to 88
was way too little
and much too late
graf had already
reclaimed its name
from the trains above
to the sub-terrain
burning BMTs
nuisance of a nation
and the IRT
gave us elevation
soon the MTA
was nearly destroyed
by the armies of the
under-employed
so the city streets
were a gallery
where the walls were sheets
and the art was free
and just like LEE said
it was not a crime
just a sign of the grime
way ahead of its time
so from top to bottom
to the end to end
we blew up the sky
like a heaven send
and our bombs were bold
though not always pretty
and when they lost control
writers went all-city
and our style was wild
while new laws were made

and though much reviled
still the vandals sprayed
and the war was fought
bombing peace by piece
or 'til we was caught by the thought police

hiphop 101

"...spitting blood clears up reality and dream alike."

—Sunao

ivory tower black power scholars
and alma mater cannon fodder
in ivy league com-brat fatigues
majoring in multi-culty
muddy mixed studies
of mystic ballistic linguistics
and last year's drop-out statistics
at privately-owned battle zone academies
where rowdy cum laude foot(note) soldiers
and under(ground) graduates
wage true or false arrest test score class war
during afternoon recess
between a thesis or a book report
on tupac vs. too short
or does little kim win against howard zinn
in moot court ski resorts
where dot com krs ones
aim rhetorical metaphorical guns
at attila the hun or big pun
just for fine-spun fun
while occasionally raging
against remedial reading
or debating the rodney king beating
and fears of a b-minus
or why the majors won't sign us
with another ancient 8 alumnus
and affirmative action fractions
from freak/greek fraternities
where intellectual emcees
with 3 degrees of separation
from sum ghetto creation
compose polemic academic
master-bation dissertations
on the rise and fall
of the hiphop nation

sharecrop hiphop

"A language comes into existence by means of brutal necessity"

— James Baldwin

stranded, branded and broken
black and brown b-boys
bartered, begged or racked back
our own home grown slum sewn,
bought or caught at cost bits
bytes beats and stolen street
cheat-sheets hacked ransacked
and mac'd way back
by caucasian contract
signed on the dotted life line
by the entwined and disinclined
clutching cut rate chewing
gum grime and not ready for prime
time last dime regurgitated rap
rhymes manu-fractured by minds
caught in decline copped,
chopped or mom and popped
by the half-price hiphop
one-stop sling-shot thrift shop
and spit swindled snippets of shit
starvation army second hand to hand
mantan disarray lay away judgment day
slavery store where any elements
from tenements and unidentified
funky objects from the projects
were jacked and scratched
free of spare part art-i-facts
on whack wax with cracked
needle tracks and then scammed
and sold with some untold
rock-n-roll and stone cold stole soul
borrowed, beaten, bruised used
and left to lose by culture vulture
hustlers and slum sample scavenger
record ravager rip-off reality rapists
escapists brothers of another murder

muttering, stuttering underlings
in underground lost and found
unnamed, chained and bound james brown
sound studios where judíos and less than zero
underclass heroes and ghetto gravedigger
new jack jigger wannabe wiggers
wield let's make a deal public eminenemy
stun gun big puns with limited funds
a-claimed and aimed to over-run
and undone the rebelushun
that's just begun

survival of the phattest

"take care not to spit against the wind"

— Friedrich Nietzsche

you said hiphop was dead
like white wonder bread
because it was universally known
that you couldn't get signed by SONY
so you threw away your demo
and canceled your chauffeur driven limo
and re-recorded your mix-tape
as a last ditch ghetto escape
and spread the word on the street
that you was the nicest on repeat

i repeat....

master of cere-moneys
or
mover of the crap
or
microphone chucker
or
model consumer
or
most co-opted
or
major capitalista...

way down all around town
uptown downtown underground
you wore the king's dookie crown
but still no-body was wanting
all the shit you was flaunting
too busy downloading for free
like the punk pirates they all be
or watching the thrown outs
on keeping it real(ity) TV
so your little hustle
was no longer worth the big hassle

and your stuper grind
had you caught in a super bind
and everybody know
you can't even buy a cup a joe
or a velvet glove
"for the love"
or a half-gallon of milk
or a suit of silk-on-silk
"on the strength"
and who wants to go to that length?
so you said to hell
with what you was tryna sell
and all the tales you was telling
because no-one ever wanted
the product you was selling
and if them niggas ain't buying
fuck that "get rich or die trying!"
so you went back to the war zone
known as your nice sub-urban home
to ask daddy for one more
badder than LL to the bone
I-got-breath-control...
no hip pop interest loan

sub-verses

"But my single desire would be to stand firm there, clinging to the last trunk... the last fighter: to die in silence"

— José Martí

how hard to speak words not hard enough to be soft
rhymes without reason tomes stripped of treason
poetry that flows like water but tastes like cheap wine
and i am dying of thirst spitting dry mouth epithets
at violent fate with a minimum-wage mouth sealed shut by
centuries of some sword-less protest
while wanting to re-write oral his-story
with pointless pencils and sabotage scrawls
snatched from pawn shop storefront graffiti
scratched on the backs of past dead porto ricans
prominently dis-played like machetero mannequins
in the plexiglass cracked rear-view mirrors
of madison avenue mausoleum museums
in money-making manhattan
still clutching rubber bullet rosaries
in lieu of real revolution with over the counter culture shock
locked on their grace-less faces
and nightshift makeshift signs
reading sealed and delivered
over the holly-wood indian head nickels
in place of their eyes that couldn't read the liner notes
in their commercialized colonized coffins
or between the front lines of fanon and magón
and bolivian diaries scribbled by secret dialectical dia-tribes
trained in guerrilla warfare by sandinista insurgents
with cuban passports stamped by fidel himself
on sacred ground touched and tilled by che and cienfuegos
while marti or marley and the i threes or assata sing
sounds of sanctified exiled blood and gunfire
lighting up the morning and i remain in mourning
torn between picking up a stun gun or a friendly pen
or spraying a claymore or krylon
words or action rhetoric or re-action
and seeds and soldiers are born and die each day
for a cause or maybe just because silence does equal deaf

words or action rhetoric or re-action

and i can't hear my own heartbeat
as i de-compose in my klepto-kindergarten composition notebooks
blank pages still searching for the write wrong words
to AGITATE, AGGRAVATE, ASSASSINATE, or lead an attack
on something more than just myself
with something more or less lethal
than these second hand-to-hand job
silenced sub-verses...

battle rhyme of the republic

"language is never neutral"

— Paulo Freire

"poetry comes from the barrel of a gun" son
words is wage slave weapons of war
and around the way AK as fuck arms
aimed to new jack attack
the heart of a slick but sick shitstem
hit them where it hurts
with a vandalized verse or worse
where you know they weakest
even the meekest emcees
must be ready to get behind
better battle rhymes
that rattle and rebel
shock and shell
reach and teach the streets
how to beat the system down
with breakbeats that burn bibles
break bones and beat them
at they own game
plan B equals booby trap raps
strategically strapped
lyrical letter bombs
sent via fed up
to blow up federal buildings
and nine millimeter mouth mines
left behind in ho chi minh
trash bins with hiphop hand-to-hand
grenade pins getting under the thin skins
of uncle psalm's cabin
stabbin' sabotage
scratches and snatched matches
struck by turntable terror wrists
in the midst of makin' musical
molotovs that breath control
rebel souls and bum rush Babylon
and on street signs where we re-write
hind-site on sight incite

turntable terror wrists
in the mist
of makin' molatovs

to fight for your right
to riot without reservations
on they radio stations
when the hiphop nations
finally re-wind the rappers'
revolt that will re-ignite
the rhyme... next time

improverbs

"This revolution is the first real creation that came out of improvisation... the most perfect example of organized chaos in the world"

— Che Guevara

freedom like philosophy
be free falling form-less
flying wild-styling within
one's soul searching
new societies' social systems
and salvation sound
that be-get up and git git down
from inside by side to break
on true to the other wide open
beside invented insurrections
off the terror-dome
ad-liberation theologies
unwritten, unarranged
and unheard holy hard
hop hieroglyphics
and his-and-her-stories
strung together loosely on
loose leaf papyrus
re-written in in-di-visible ink
like the missing link
to the funk that still stink
swinging sub-version x-cursions
jammin' into jury-rigged
jump start jazz clubs
and cryptic cre-old churches
of the creators, innovators
where the profit-less prophets
read in-coded odes
while playing tracks of found facts
for the swaying gods of violence
while art-pocalyptic originators
improvise psalms in their own
out loud silence

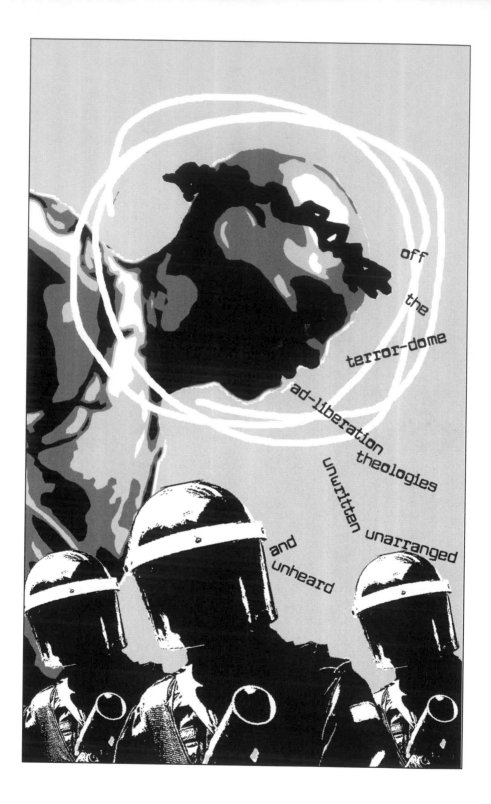

prophetic poetics
(a high coup)

"It is difficult to get the news from poems, yet men die miserably every day for lack of what is found there"

— William Carlos Williams

And when it comes down
put down your paper and pen
spic pick up a gun

grab a stick or stone
because poems can't break bone
or smash! bash! destroy!

words make weak weapons
and a sonnet will not kill
never has nor will

rock razor scissors
make sure they be nice and sharp
knives cut to the chase

only keep pencils
if their point is a dagger
to leave a deep wound

throw out all papers
or let 'em burn baby burn
along with yo books

cuz rhymes can't do the crime
and letters never help you
to spell seize the time

attica again(st)
(for kakamia)

"With the exception of Indian massacres in the late 19th century, the State Police assault which ended the four-day prison uprising was the bloodiest one-day encounter between Americans since the Civil War."

— New York State Special Commission on Attica

blood red in my eye
painting pictures
spic scriptures
across concrete
canvas walls
30 feet high
2 feet thick
tick tick tick
nigger sticks
beating down
in surround sound
in the prison compound
and all along the gun tower
this final hour
stifled shouts for black power(!)
a bucket or a shower
and toilet tissue were the only issue
for a second rate inmate
somewhere upstate
brandishing empty hands
and a simple list of demands
but god damn the man
this may be my last stand
and one man's riot
is a thousand strong
rebel song...
ATTICA!
ATTICA!
ATTICA!
shank held tightly between thumb and index finger
a simple slice across skin and vein
offering officers with slit throats in exchange

and one mans riot
is a thousand strong
rebel song...

for my dashed hopes held like hostages
between heaven or san quentin
george jackson or rockefeller's re-action
up against the wall 'till the last man fall
mutherfucker! this ain't no tv
and I intend to get free
this be inmate justice....
and they said you can trust us
but the governor was a liar
as the stormtroopers opened fire

common rebellion in progress
(for the real warriors)

"PIGS: if you all think you're supermen, unity is kryptonite"

— Jesús Papoleto Meléndez

can you dig it!
ghettos! gutters! gulags!
barrios! favelas! jungles!
shanties! slums! streets!
have you heard the news?
latin kings without crowns be throwin' down
Young lords without land are fighting the man
Bishops without flocks is killing cops
can you count! 25,000 strong nationwide!
800,000 deep side by side!
500 latino gangs in LA alone
20,000 asian gangs in amerika
75 blood sets set it off!
200 crip cliques! click.... BOOM!
bounty hunters
shotguns eight trey watts, LA
nomads don't take turf fight for what it's worth
force freedom
disciples follow for now
and once you know how lead tomorrow
stop YAPing start capping
stone cold savage skulls of old
crazy homicides! along for the ride!
rebel souls!
dragons!
viceroys!
DDP!
SWP !
ñetas!
maras!
mongrel mobs!
apaches with haches!
BLACK POWER!
BLACK POWER!
BLACK POWER!

read the hazard sign
trouble makers get in line
earth-shakers
mayhem-makers
autonomy-takers
they have 35,000 pigs by day
patrolling the Bronx zoo
we've got infinite spades at night
waiting to decide what to do
SET IT OFF!
SET IT OFF!
SET IT OFF!
you can win with discipline
if you are dedicated!
if you are organized!
if you are united!
if you are smart!
if you are ready!
if you are real!
if you can count!!!

we

seized
the
time

we slung puerto punk rocks

setting fascist
forts on fire
and sending
slave wage smoke
signals to the
other souljahs

puerto punk rocks

"we are poets even when we don't write poems."

— Nikki Giovanni

we wasn't no poets so instead of words
we slung puerto punk rocks at private property
public nuisance number one in a million
casting primitive weapons at bullet proof skyscrapers
thin arms marked with dirt
taíno tattoos flailing like it was our first fistfight
armed struggle with stones and brittle bones
breaking and entering into enemy homes
it felt like freedom when we hit the fortress façade
fist held high, feet in motion
running from scale security soldiers
with our brown chavo-che-guevara baby faces covered
by black masks like some slum subcomandante Marcos
of manhattan moving through the corporate chain store concertina
and the high-priced highrise hell fire and brimstones
that the builder refused in our cargo pockets
running fast past the mansions and white men walking black dogs
smashing and slashing seditious slogans
on swept shit stink stained sidewalks
setting fascist forts on fire and sending slave wage smoke signals
to the other souljahs as we stole survival scraps
from starvation army de-concentration camps
dived into dumpsters like they was luquillo beach cliffs
and raced like rebel rats through alleys and gutters and ghettos
through the barbwire barrios passed the politrick pigs
patrolling city street cell block shell shock eye in the sky slums
with gas masks and govern-mental guns pointed point blank
at nigga native suns running fast passed ku klux klan sweat shop
kops and colonial clampdown caretakers and factory funeral
prison processions in session tagging our economic epitaph
on invisible walls as we raced towards temporary autonomous
project halls swift as city sandinista sidewalk zapatistas
dodging bullets like ballet b-boys improvising, strategizing
and fantasizing an uptown uprising

we seized the time, if only in our mind
empty bellies in knots
nostrils scorched with gas
and gun smoke
eyes wet from laughter and tears

reclaim the streets

"To stay free is theoretical. It is to take over your immediate environment"

— Miguel Algarín

they all left on the A train headed downtown
hoping to hop the connection to the gravy train
which didn't stop in the get-o-ver any more
all their names had been changed to correct the reticent
these black and brown bodies crammed in a sardine can
headed towards heaven or at least out of harlem
in secondhand me down suits bought with lawsuits
taken out on landlords who never removed the lead paint
in their SROs fit for a family of five including little jesus
who wasn't so little anymore but never really grew up
or out as out they went jumping turnstyles in style
over the ghetto and past the hoods
holding the door to get in a few more and in they went
on their way out cursing the conductor
as the train traveled thru the loco line
that wasn't fast enough to outpace hell or the starving hounds
that roamed thru the barrio streets like fossils found
just feet away from a stale crumb chewed into sub-mission
by soldier ants with attitudes who battled rats in kevlar
made from campbell's soup cans to protect themselves
from the upscale army who traveled in cars
crafted from corporate coffins that were begged or borrowed
from the mortuary mall with plastic slave master ID cards
that identified their debt to society that they never planned to pay
along with the tickets they received for driving outside
of the handicapped parking battle zones that surrounded the slum
like concertina cops keeping in the inmates doing life bids
while they waited to be pardoned for living
while inside jesus organized a cell in his cell
pacing in combat boots that still had their soles
because he'd never sold his

to burn and loot and dance and sing

while inside jesus organized a call in his cell

and now he ran an insurrection from within
with all dem who would remain nameless
who hadn't yet left and had nowhere else to go
and were left behind unshackled unshaken and unhinged
to bum rush burn and loot and dance and sing and swing
on deserted streets that were now reclaimed

last of the po' ricans (the great dying part dos)

"His remembrance shall perish from this earth and he shall have no name in the street. He shall be driven from light into darkness, and chased out of the world"

—Job 18:17-18

...and i re-mained, like the last left rican-structed casita on some anonymous esquina as the former sometimes spanish harlem aka SPAHA came tumbling down not unlike the likes of a lonely domino player or a nodding tecato as the first last affordable refurbished billion dollar luxury condo called the san juan stonehenge was constructed atop the rubble and rabble along the former Julia de Burgos blvd where the welfare warehouses used to be lined up along long before the mass last exit slash exodus i.e. excavation anti-poverty project was in full swing just across the hit or miss-calibrated calle where the former fonda boricua used to deal in goya beans and last ditch schemes for cheap or free but was now an under-cover staples or something selling gold graffitti-embossed lost and found calling cards at almost cost to compete with the costco deconcentration camp community land bust that was once east harlem café or carlitos cuchifrito kiosk on the other corner by the former camaradas that was now the russian mafia tea room where the ex el barrio museo now known as manteca museum was con-currently filled with mourners, mormons and other climb the ladder day saints and sinners trying to goodbye, bug or beg a won way ticket out of harlem or here or back into hell or some low income housing cells that were no longer for sale as i-very towers had long ago replaced orishas or any other afro-rican powers and young land-lords had already seized the hour of our discontent granting evictions in lieu of predictions hand to handed out outside the best-buy botanicá that had become a burial ground down to zero plus one native son of a made in american gun hidden in a macy's red-star dime-bag gang rag that used to be la marqueta with no place to buy bullets bartering for balas outside la bodega bloomingdales that became ponce de león bank became citibank became bank of america of the un-united nations and the chase was on mi casa was now their condo and the revolution would now be gentrified as latino lemmings were led face first into the east river the 51st real estate boom was our latest greatest and last porto rican eulogy written in blood money wooden nickels and rubber food stamp

cruz-i-fictional afflictions for the term-anal addictions to speaking in
rican or being sorta poor-ta-pitiful while in amerika the bootiful

... and still I stayed behind in time out-of-my-mind because I was all
that was left or right in the middle of a ghost in the machine town
uptown was now downtown which was a suburb of somewhere else
where street signs showed the way to the last first exit out of here,
there and anywhere aquí no se habla español 3D day glo bill-boreds
shouted like out loud wide awake nightmares and I had finally learned
to read between the graffiti and street signs of the crimes this time
on every side streets where I couldn't even get a sideways glance or a
second first last chance to declare that I was really still there ever at
all and the last exit suicide note written in broken spanglitch by a half-
dead cockroach from the corner chino-latino take-out on a partially
chewed con' flake crumb that read or said no mo po' ricans here / hear
or anywhere else either at last

but I was the last at last...

el fin.

AFTERWORD

Art After Words

It ain't where you're from it's where you're at.

—Rakim

It's not where you take things from - it's where you take them to.

—Jean Luc Godard

BEGINNINGS ARE HARD TO PIN DOWN. Where does *Last Of The Po'Ricans y Otros Afro-artifacts* begin? Did it begin with Not-4Prophet writing poems on walls as a young graffiti artist? Yes. Did it begin when the longer pieces he began writing went from walls to composition notebooks? Yes. Did it begin when those poems became lyrics? Yes. Did it begin when Not4Prophet and I met in the nineties when he was the lead vocalist and lyricist of the Nuyorican punk band RICANSTRUCTION? Yes. Did it begin when we collaborated on those first three chapbooks? Yes. *Last Of The Po'Ricans Y Otros Afro-artifacts* began there and there and there and it kept beginning over and over again until it became what you now hold in your hands. Like all things Nuyorican, the taproots are always plural, never singular, and one must sift through the afro-artifacts of the last Po'Ricans to find them. Like I said, beginnings are hard to pin down.

For me it began when I met Not4Prophet and the political artistic aesthetic home he and his band RICANSTRUCTION created for me. The music was an eclectic kitchen sink mix of salsa, be-bop, reggae and hip-hop built around the framework of hardcore punk. Imagine the joyful noise of Willie Colón, John Coltrane, Bob Marley, Public Enemy and the Bad Brains and you begin to get a sense of what RICANSTRUCTION sounded like. As lead vocalist and lyricist, Not4Prophet drew from similarly eclectic sources that ran the gamut from Miguel Piñero to John Lennon, from Joe Strummer to Chuck D, from Amiri Baraka, Curtis Mayfield and Nina Simone to Bob Marley and Bob Dylan.

RICANSTRUCTION's aggressive performances, in their recordings and in their live performances led by Not4Prophet, tapped into something both musically and lyrically that inspired people. It became a voice that stood for something in an artistic, political and lyrical sense that grew into something beyond just being a band. Other artists were attracted to the possibilities that RICANSTRUCTION inspired and projects outside of the band's recordings and live shows began to take shape. In an effort to try and define the space that was being carved out by this new aesthetic, we created the RICANSTRUCTION Netwerk. Politics and art merged within the Netwerk and a large part of the ethos that drove this was an anti-corporate DIY aesthetic. A variety of projects went from conception to execution: protests and political education classes, agit-prop production, painting illegal murals, graffiti campaigns, postering campaigns, pamphlets, the 'zine *Salvo*, and avant-garde music videos and films.

It was during this time that Not4Prophet asked me if I would create some graphics for his poetry chapbook, and I quickly agreed because I believed his poetry was fertile ground for visual imagery. Not4Prophet builds lucid surrealistic visuals from his words, and as esoteric as they initially seem, there is a tangible and visceral quality to his work that lives and breathes. *Subverses* is the first chapbook we did together; it is kind of a primer for the breadth of Not4Prophet's poetry. The next chapbook, *Resistance 101,* is a collection of Puerto Rican liberation poems. This volume was followed by *Thrift Shop Hip Hop,* a collection of street poetry. We made these chapbooks old-school, reminiscent of the poets/political activists from the 1960s; we photocopied, folded and saddle-stitched the books ourselves. They were an intoxicating and combustible mixture of Anarcho politics, Nuyorican roots, Black Arts aesthetics, Puerto Rican nationalism, hip-hop street credibility and righteous punk anger.

From the very beginning, creating images for Not4Prophet's poetry required a new way of thinking for me. Up until that point, I had done graffiti, drawings, painting, murals, photography and filmmaking, but I had never illustrated a book. The work I'd been doing before I got into doing the graphics for these poems was designing and creating flyers, handbills and posters for band gigs and political protests. That work required a kind of visually striking simplicity that needed to grab people's attention away from the corporate bombardment they experienced daily. By the time I began working on Not4Prophet's chapbooks, I was able to bring this newly acquired aesthetic to another level with graphically stimulating material that didn't have to compete for people's attention.

I was inspired to work in collage because the diverse imagery Not4Prophet conjures up in his poetry breaks form and represents different sounds and textures. And instead of physically cutting and gluing materials, I did it digitally, stripping the color from photos and cutting out the background to create a simplified space so I could layer the images. In some cases, I degraded the images so that the graphics have an old-school punk 'zine or hip-hop flyer feel to them. I wanted the artwork to have a high contrast, black and white, badly photocopied quality, as if they were artifacts of a by-gone era discarded in a box under a mattress that's found by some future urban archeologist.

I also incorporated short bursts of verse from Not4Prophet's poems. These few lines were like trailers for a movie designed to entice. These images are inextricably connected to the poems because of those lines of poetry. If the graphics were ever separated from the poems it would be like some damaged ancient artifact hinting at some deeper mystery.

Besides Not4Prophet's poetry, I was also influenced by some really great artists I've admired over the years. I became a fan of Gee Vaucher when she was doing the covers for English Anarcho-punk band CRASS, which looked like photographic surreal collages but were actually paintings made to look that way. I also was a fan of the collage art of Winston Smith, who did many of the covers for the DEAD KENNEDYS. The work of Jean-Michel Basquiat was something that made its presence known, not so much in his painting technique but in his use of complex layered imagery and text. Early punk and hip-hop flyers and magazines, and the style in which they were laid out, were another influence that began to surface when creating these graphics. I reclaimed and repurposed images with the layered effect of a graffiti-strewn wall. I think my overall guiding influence was graffiti. These seemingly disparate artistic influences only reinforced each other in my mind as they all shared a desire to peel back the layers of illusion as so much of Not4Prophet's poetry does.

Not4Prophet and I share a sensibility in many of these influences, not only graphic in nature, but also musically driven as so much of Not4Prophet's poetry is. Which brings us back to beginnings and where and how did *Last Of The Po'Ricans Y Otros Afro-artifacts* begin? Did it begin with the liberation that graffiti brought two Nuyoricans? Yes. Did it begin with two Nuyoricans tripping over punk? Yes. Did it begin when that punk and hip-hop ethos shaped their sensibilities? Yes. It began there and there and there as well.

The thing about beginnings is that they can be traced back further and further, but beginnings eventually do come to an end and I suppose that the publication of *Last Of The Po'Ricans y Otros Afro-artifacts* marks the end of that beginning. No matter where you decide to place the beginning of this book, it cannot be argued that it didn't begin out of a passion to create something unique. If you look beyond the ink and between the lines, you'll see these pages are soaked with DNA in the form of blood, spit, sweat, tears and love born out of Not4Prophet's poems.

It was an honor to be a part of it. ❊

—vagabond
filmmaker, artist and agitator

ABOUT THE POET

PHOTO: Sam Lahoz

NOT4PROPHET was born in Ponce, Puerto Rico and raised in East Harlem and the South Bronx in New York City. He is a hardcore Hip Hop MC, political Punk Rocker, graffiti writer, and a dirt-roots community organizer.

He first began performing music and improvising poetry at squats and community gardens in the Lower East Side/Loisaida, NYC in the mid-1990s, and founded the Puerto Rican anarcho-independentista arts collective known as Ricanstruction Netwerk during that time.

Not4Prophet has released several indie music CDs with his bands, Ricanstruction, Renegades of Punk, and X-Vandals, and his writing has appeared in various books and magazines, including *Let Fury Have the Hour, Letters from Young Activists, The Quotable Rebel, The Centro Journal, Scrawl Magazine, Ugly Planet, TAO Noise, ipropaganda Magazine,* and the self published *Salvo 'zine.*

Today, the "not for profit" Prophet is recognized and respected in underground, independent music circles as a staunch anti-corporate avenger, activist and artists, and as the visionary behind an anti-corporate street HipHop movement known as AGIT (All Ghetto Indigenous Tribes) Army. He also currently teaches "resistance writing" at the Homeless Organizing Academy in the South Bronx, and continues to diligently organize and agitate (in) the hood. www.agitarmy.org. ❈

ABOUT THE ARTIST

PHOTO: Jeffrey Akers

VAGABOND is a filmmaker and multi-disciplinary artist who was born in Brooklyn to Puerto Rican and Jamaican parents. A graduate of Fiorello H. LaGuardia High School of Music & the Arts, he attended The School of Visual Arts but dropped out after his first year to work on indcpendent black films such as Spikes Lee's *Do The Right Thing,* where he quickly learned all aspects of filmmaking and forged his own alternative aesthetic.

vagabond has written, produced and directed the documentary *Ricanstructing Vieques,* and the award-winning feature film, *Machetero.* A former member of the RICANSTRUCTION Netwerk, a politically radical artist collective in the vein of the "Situationist International," he continues to work on films, create posters, pamphlets, videos and all kinds of other agit-propaganda for "the cause" or just because. www.nothngtobegainedhere.com

OTHER BOOKS BY 2LEAF PRESS

2LEAF PRESS challenges the status quo by publishing alternative fiction, non-fiction, poetry and bilingual works by activists, academics, poets and authors dedicated to diversity and social justice with scholarship that is accessible to the general public. 2LEAF PRESS produces high quality and beautifully produced hardcover, paperback and ebook formats through our series: *2LP Explorations in Diversity, 2LP University Books, 2LP Classics, 2LP Translations, Nuyorican World Series,* and *2LP Current Affairs, Culture & Politics.* Below is a selection of 2LEAF PRESS' published titles.

2LP EXPLORATIONS IN DIVERSITY

Substance of Fire: Gender and Race in the College Classroom
by Claire Millikin
Foreword by R. Joseph Rodríguez, Afterword by Richard Delgado
Contributed material by Riley Blanks, Blake Calhoun, Rox Trujillo

Black Lives Have Always Mattered
A Collection of Essays, Poems, and Personal Narratives
Edited by Abiodun Oyewole

The Beiging of America:
Personal Narratives about Being Mixed Race in the 21st Century
Edited by Cathy J. Schlund-Vials, Sean Frederick Forbes, Tara Betts
with an Afterword by Heidi Durrow

What Does it Mean to be White in America?
Breaking the White Code of Silence, A Collection of Personal Narratives
Edited by Gabrielle David and Sean Frederick Forbes
Introduction by Debby Irving and Afterword by Tara Betts

2LP UNIVERSITY BOOKS
Designs of Blackness, Mappings in the Literature and
Culture of African Americans
A. Robert Lee
20TH ANNIVERSARY EXPANDED EDITION

2LP CLASSICS
Adventures in Black and White
Edited and with a critical introduction by Tara Betts
by Philippa Duke Schuyler

Monsters: Mary Shelley's Frankenstein and Mathilda
by Mary Shelley, edited by Claire Millikin Raymond

2LP TRANSLATIONS
Birds on the Kiswar Tree
by Odi Gonzales, Translated by Lynn Levin
Bilingual: English/Spanish

Incessant Beauty, A Bilingual Anthology
by Ana Rossetti, Edited and Translated by Carmela Ferradáns
Bilingual: English/Spanish

NUYORICAN WORLD SERIES
Our Nuyorican Thing, The Birth of a Self-Made Identity
by Samuel Carrion Diaz, with an Introduction by Urayoán Noel
Bilingual: English/Spanish

Hey Yo! Yo Soy!, 40 Years of Nuyorican Street Poetry,
The Collected Works of Jesús Papoleto Meléndez
Bilingual: English/Spanish

LITERARY NONFICTION
No Vacancy; Homeless Women in Paradise
by Michael Reid

The Beauty of Being, A Collection of Fables, Short Stories & Essays
by Abiodun Oyewole

WHEREABOUTS: Stepping Out of Place,
An Outside in Literary & Travel Magazine Anthology
Edited by Brandi Dawn Henderson

PLAYS
Rivers of Women, The Play
by Shirley Bradley LeFlore, with photographs by Michael J. Bracey

AUTOBIOGRAPHIES/MEMOIRS/BIOGRAPHIES
Trailblazers, Black Women Who Helped Make America Great
American Firsts/American Icons
by Gabrielle David

Mother of Orphans
The True and Curious Story of Irish Alice, A Colored Man's Widow
by Dedria Humphries Barker

Strength of Soul
by Naomi Raquel Enright

Dream of the Water Children:
Memory and Mourning in the Black Pacific
by Fredrick D. Kakinami Cloyd
Foreword by Velina Hasu Houston, Introduction by Gerald Horne
Edited by Karen Chau

The Fourth Moment: Journeys from the Known to the Unknown, A Memoir
by Carole J. Garrison, Introduction by Sarah Willis

POETRY
PAPOLíTICO, Poems of a Political Persuasion
by Jesús Papoleto Meléndez
with an Introduction by Joel Kovel and DeeDee Halleck

Critics of Mystery Marvel, Collected Poems
by Youssef Alaoui, with an Introduction by Laila Halaby

shrimp
by jason vasser-elong, with an Introduction by Michael Castro
The Revlon Slough, New and Selected Poems
by Ray DiZazzo, with an Introduction by Claire Millikin

Written Eye: Visuals/Verse
by A. Robert Lee

A Country Without Borders: Poems and Stories of Kashmir
by Lalita Pandit Hogan, with an Introduction by Frederick Luis Aldama

Branches of the Tree of Life
The Collected Poems of Abiodun Oyewole 1969-2013
by Abiodun Oyewole, edited by Gabrielle David
with an Introduction by Betty J. Dopson

2Leaf Press is an imprint owned and operated by the Intercultural Alliance of Artists & Scholars, Inc. (IAAS), a NY-based nonprofit organization that publishes and promotes multicultural literature.

NEW YORK
www.2leafpress.org